small talk

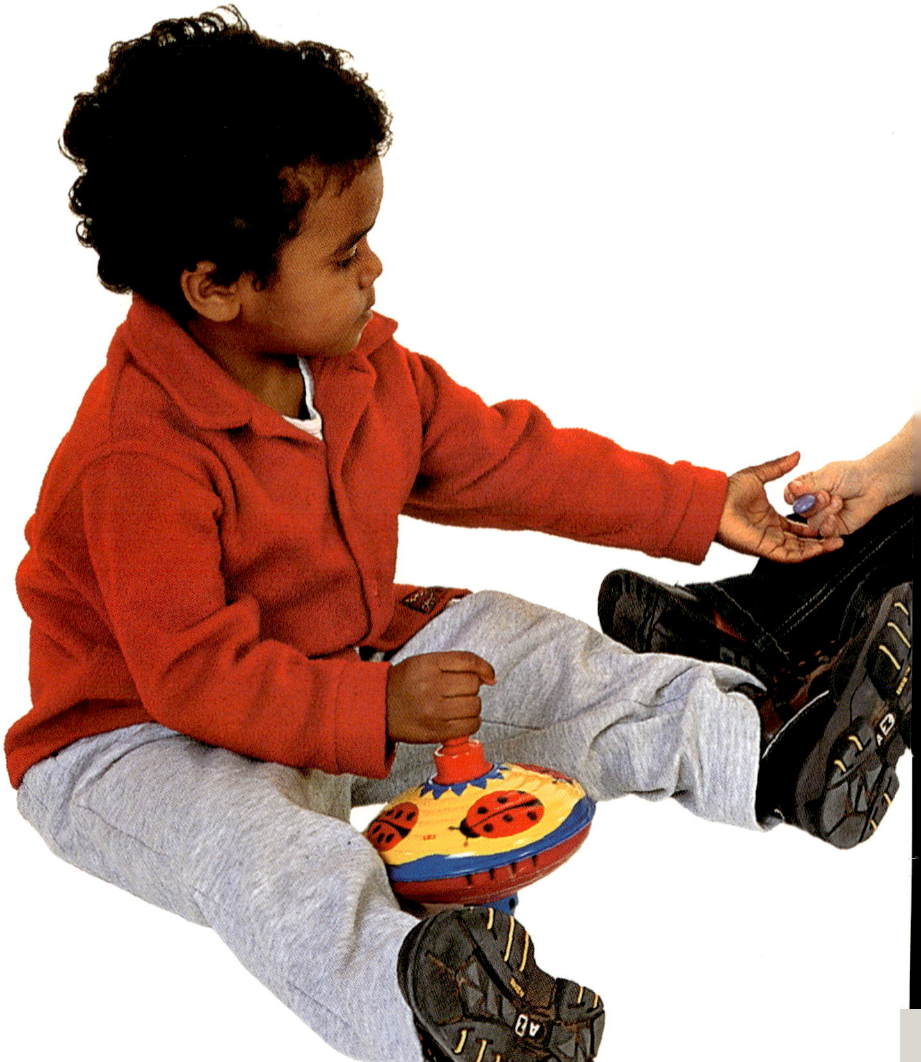

small talk

Dr. Richard C. Woolfson

BARRON'S

First edition for North America published by
Barron's Educational Series, Inc., 2002.

First published 2002
under the title SMALL TALK by Hamlyn, an imprint,
part of Octopus Publishing Group Ltd, 2-4 Heron
Quays, Docklands, London E14 4JP, Great Britain

American edition Copyright © 2002 by
Barron's Educational Series, Inc.

Copyright © 2002 by Octopus Publishing Group Limited

All rights reserved.
No part of this book may be reproduced
in any form, by photostat, microfilm,
xerography, or any other means, or
incorporated into any information
retrieval system, electronic or
mechanical, without the written
permission of the copyright owner.

All inquiries should be addressed to:
Barron's Educational Series, Inc.
250 Wireless Boulevard
Hauppauge, New York 11788
http://www.barronseduc.com

International Standard Book
Number 0-7641-1881-1

Library of Congress Catalog
Card No. 2001092582

Printed in China

9 8 7 6 5 4 3 2 1

Contents

FOREWORD 6

INTRODUCTION 8

		Language Development	Body Language	Top Tips	Questions and Answers	Development Chart
0–3 months	20	22	24	26	28	30
4–6 months	32	34	36	38	40	42
7–9 months	44	46	48	50	52	54
10–12 months	56	58	60	62	64	66
13–15 months	68	70	72	74	76	78
16–18 months	80	82	84	86	88	90
19–21 months	92	94	96	98	100	102
22–24 months	104	106	108	110	112	114
25–30 months	116	118	120	122	124	126
31–36 months	128	130	132	134	136	138

INDEX 140

ACKNOWLEDGMENTS 144

Foreword

Being a parent is exciting. Of course, it's also very hard work, but the thrill of forming a strong bond between you and your growing child makes it all worthwhile. Knowing that you connect with each other gives you immense satisfaction and pleasure, and it also makes your baby feel safe, secure, and loved.

Effective communication is a fundamental part of that crucial bonding process, whether it's the ability to comfort your crying baby, to stimulate your infant's language skills, to calm your angry toddler, to have a conversation with your young child, or to help your preschooler solve a difficult challenge. Communication with your child is the foundation of your relationship with each other.

And that's where this book comes in. By explaining all about the development and understanding of both spoken language and body language, it empowers you to enhance your child's communication skills with you and others—both children and adults—and enables you to improve your own communication skills with your growing child.

It's not simply about encouraging your child to speak, though that's vital. And it's not simply about learning how to interpret your child's facial expressions and gestures, though that's vital, too. It's really about helping the two of you to form a close bond with each other. And when you do establish effective communication, you and your child will become much closer, much more at ease in each other's company—and you'll both feel much more fulfilled.

Richard C. Woolfson

Introduction

9

Understanding Spoken Language

Language Dimensions

The development in your child's language as she grows from a new baby, whose only sound is a distressed cry, to a talking, communicating (and possibly argumentative!) 3-year-old who can ask questions, offer her opinion, disagree with you and hold a conversation is one of the most remarkable features of this period in childhood.

Psychologists studying language development have identified four key dimensions:

- **Language sounds**

These are the individual sounds, syllables, words, and sentences that your child speaks. Also known as "phonology," this refers to your child's actual speech sounds. As she grows she progresses from the incoherent babbling of a baby to the clear sentences of a 3-year-old.

- **Language meaning**

Virtually all your child's spoken language carries meaning. True, there are times when as a baby she makes a noise just for the sake of it, but most of her sounds, syllables, and words mean something specific. This aspect of language is also called "semantic."

- **Language grammar**

Language follows a system of rules: for instance, that word types appear in a certain order in a sentence, that there are pronouns and prepositions, singulars and plurals, and so on. Referred to as "syntax," grammar is the structure of your child's sentences.

- **Language context**

Aside from words, language also involves social rules, such as taking turns in conversation, listening while the other person speaks, and modifying vocabulary according to the situation and people involved. Awareness of these social rules is also known as "pragmatics."

You'll find that your child's language progresses along all of these dimensions, initially only in terms of sounds and meaning but soon in terms of grammar and social context as well.

Above and left This little girl's development from a crying newborn to a confident toddler is evident not only in her physical coordination but also in her communication skills.

Below Even though this baby cannot form coherent words, she can make her feelings known and respond to basic instructions.

Above Soothing words will help to comfort your new baby. Your gentle intonations will begin to register as positive sounds.

RECEPTIVE AND EXPRESSIVE LANGUAGE

There is a difference between the language your child hears and understands (receptive language) and the language she is able to produce herself (expressive language). Both these aspects progress considerably in the first three years of life.

With virtually all children, receptive language outstrips expressive language. In other words, your child understands a lot more than she can say at almost every stage of development. During the first year, for instance, when she has no individual words that she can say clearly, she understands many common, everyday words that you use—you can tell this by her reaction when you say them to her. When she reaches 3 years old, she understands very complex sentences that you use even though she is unable to make and speak these same sentences herself.

THEORIES OF LANGUAGE DEVELOPMENT

Psychologists disagree when it comes to explaining how language develops in children, and the key disagreement rests on the different roles of heredity and environment. Like all nature-versus-nurture debates, opinions are divided.

The "nature" group of language theorists claims that every child is born with an innate ability to learn language, that she is preprogrammed to learn verbal communication. That's why the milestones of language are so similar across all children—after all, nobody learns to talk in grammatically correct sentences before they speak single words. If language was affected by environment, these theorists continue, then every child would learn language in a unique way because of her unique environment. This natural ability to learn language shows with the baby's first cry and grows from that moment onward.

The "nurture" group of psychologists take an opposing view, maintaining that a child's language develops from imitating the words she hears in her everyday life, and through parental reinforcement when she speaks. For instance, the parent says the word "mama," which the infant manages to repeat; at that point the parent smiles broadly, encouraging the child to say the word again. In this way, claim these theorists, language is heavily influenced by environment.

Perhaps the best approach—and the one adopted in this book—is to assume that nature and nurture both play a part. Common sense and everyday experience as a parent provide evidence for this assumption. Environment obviously plays a part, because a child raised in an English-speaking family learns to speak English, not Italian, and a child raised in an Italian-speaking family learns to speak Italian, not English. On the other hand, a child creates new words of her own, such as "wenteded" (instead of "went"), words that she has never heard before. This demonstrates that she thinks about basic language rules and then applies them in innovative ways.

It's hard to compare the role of "nature" against the role of "nurture," but in reality you don't really need to know. What matters is that you provide a stimulating environment for your child at home, one in which spoken and written language play a significant part. Competence in understanding and speaking language enables your growing child to enrich her life—socially, emotionally, and intellectually—so it's worth making this a parenting priority.

Below Verbal and visual stimulation play a vital role in the development of your child. Picture books are an ideal starting point.

Understanding Body Language

Why Body Language?

You use body language all the time and so does your child, even though you probably don't consciously think about it. You smile at your child when you are happy with him and he smiles back; that's body language. You frown when you're annoyed at your child and he pouts in response; that's body language. In other words, body language—the meaning conveyed by body movements, such as gaze, facial expression, and touch—is part of your daily life.

Above A happy response to your smile is always encouraging.

The more you and your growing child understand each other's nonverbal communication, the closer your relationship becomes. That's only one of the reasons this book focuses on body language. Here are two more:

Body language is used more than spoken language. Studies comparing the amount of spoken with nonverbal language exchanged between two people in a relationship have found that body language dominates. Results of such studies show that less than 10 percent of emotions are expressed in words, whereas more than 90 percent are expressed in body language. At 3 years old, your child is more likely to use words to communicate facts and body language to communicate emotions.

Body language is less controlled than spoken language. In most instances, your child makes a decision to speak words. His speech may be impulsive at times, but generally he says what he thinks. Body language is less easily controlled. Smiles, body posture, leg and arm movements, eye contact, and other features of nonverbal communication occur without deliberate planning. This means that your child's body language seeps out, even though he doesn't realize it. Interpreting his body language, therefore, gives you a good insight into his underlying feelings.

Below and left This child at 7 months and again at 19 months has a happy disposition, which is evident in her facial expression and general body language.

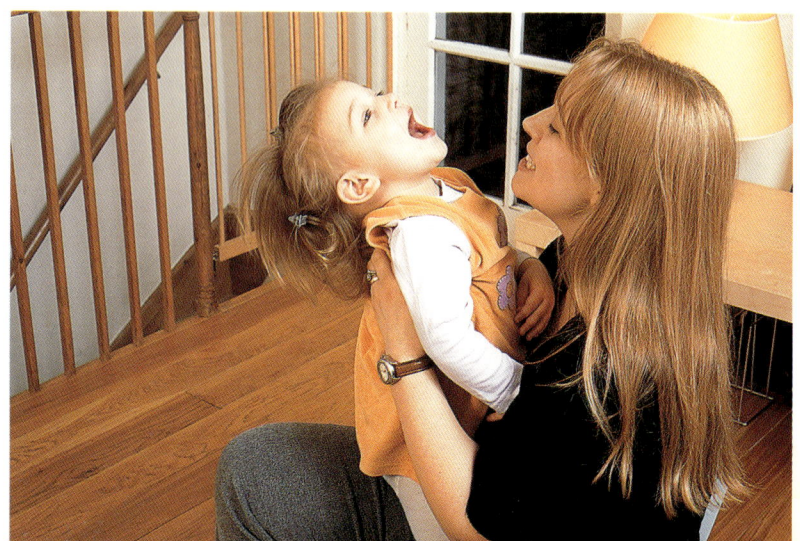

DIMENSIONS OF BODY LANGUAGE

Although the interpretation of body language is often very complicated—estimates suggest there are more than a million different gestures and expressions that convey meaning—there is nothing to keep you from understanding the basics. And that alone will improve your relationship with your child, right from the start.

This book examines the elementary components of nonverbal communication, which are:

- **Face** As soon as he is born, your baby starts to make facial expressions that reflect his inner feelings. By the time he is 3 years old he has a wide variety of expressions that tell you something about his underlying emotions.
- **Eyes** Eye contact is a natural part of human communication; instinctively, we look into each other's eyes during a conversation. Variations in the rate of eye contact can indicate anything from fascination to guilt.
- **Stance** Once your toddler starts to move around, you'll notice he adopts various postures—for instance, the one that tells you he is sad because he moves slowly with hunched shoulders.
- **Hands and fingers** If you notice that your child's hands are gripped tightly shut in a fist, you can be sure he's angry and upset. But if they are open, dangling casually by his sides, then he is probably relaxed.
- **Legs** A child who shifts backward and forward from one foot to the other is usually concerned about something. He may feel guilty about what he is saying at the time, or perhaps he is afraid.
- **Breathing** Rate of breathing often changes as a result of emotional state. Quick, shallow breathing is associated with nervousness, whereas deep, slow breaths can be a reflection of your child's relaxation.
- **Distance** When he is in a bad mood, your child creates distance between you and him, perhaps by sitting on the opposite side of the room. On the other hand, he likes to snuggle up close to you when he feels anxious about something.

MAKING A START

When trying to understand your child's body language, remember that this is not an exact science! You probably won't get it right every time.

The best way to improve your skill in this area is through accumulated experience of watching your child closely in a variety of situations. For instance, when he is a baby you'll soon know when you have interpreted the meaning of his cries accurately, because you'll be able to ease his distress. And when he is a child, you can test out the accuracy of your interpretations by simply asking him what he feels. So, spend time observing your child.

Another way to improve your ability to understand nonverbal communication is by looking at other people. For instance, you could watch a television program with the volume turned off, so that you can see the main characters without hearing their words. Try to figure out what they "say" to each other, solely on the basis of their body language. Or watch other people in the street. You'll be amazed at how much you can deduce from body language alone once you build up your confidence and experience.

Above By interpreting her baby's body language and distressed cry this mother has detected the source of irritation and made her baby more comfortable.

The Importance of Stimulation

Stimulating Spoken Language

From the moment she is born, your child has a natural instinct to communicate with you. That cry she makes when entering the world is her first means of connecting with those outside her, and it continues from there on. She wants to communicate with you—there is little doubt that she is preprogrammed to develop spoken language. But she still needs help to fulfill this language potential, and that's why your stimulation matters.

Bear in mind that language activities should be fun, for both you and your child, and should occur informally. It's not a case of having a planned program of speech exercises containing a set number of activities each day—that is likely to bore both you and your child! Most of the suggestions and ideas for stimulating your child's spoken language given in this book can be carried out as part of her normal daily routine.

Language occurs all around your child, whether it is the sound of you talking to her or to someone else, the sounds she hears on the radio and television, the stories she has read to her, or the voices of children playing together. She hears spoken language all the time. Through the natural process of language development, she responds to this stimulation, using it to improve her own spoken language. So try to find a balance between naturally occurring language experiences and planned language activities. This book offers you advice on both these strategies.

STIMULATING BODY LANGUAGE

The same general principles apply to body language. With nonverbal communication, however, your main aim will be to improve your understanding of it (and her understanding of it, too), rather than specifically extending her repertoire of body language.

In other words, your child's interest in body language is stimulated by the knowledge that you understand her hidden messages—and that she understands yours. To achieve this goal, you need to grasp the main elements of her nonverbal communication and then use that understanding purposefully so that she becomes closer to you.

The suggestions given in this book about nonverbal communication will guide you through the complexities of this form of communication that flows between you and your child. Keep it fun, and don't worry if you cannot understand all of her gestures. Your skills in this area

Above You can make speech exercises fun by singing songs and letting your child play along with a musical instrument.

will improve with time, experience, and practice.

A HOLISTIC APPROACH

Language and communication skills represent only one area of your child's development. As you'll read in this book, there are other areas, such as hand-eye coordination skills, movement skills, learning skills, and social and emotional skills. Progress in all these different areas—not just in language and communication alone—combine to make your growing child the very special and unique individual she is.

So, avoid the temptation to concentrate exclusively on spoken language and body language while ignoring her needs in these other areas. Of course you want your child to have good speech and language,

Below Playing ball games and participating in other physical activities with your child will help his overall development.

Bottom Your child's spoken language will improve in small-group situations where he begins to learn the rudiments of conversation.

but you also want her to learn new things all the time, to get on well with other children, and to be able to enjoy physical activities that involve hand, arm, and leg movements. Encourage progress in your child's overall development and not only her language.

Another reason for taking a holistic approach to stimulating your child is that each area of development interacts with the others. For instance, playing with other children improves her spoken language, because children spontaneously talk to each other; concentrating on a small jigsaw puzzle improves your child's hand-eye coordination while encouraging her to talk to you about the challenge she wants to complete. Virtually everything you do with her stimulates more than one dimension of her development at the same time.

This means that language stimulation takes place nearly all the time, no matter what you and your child do together. The activities given in this book should fit in comfortably and naturally with your child's day-to-day routine.

TIME TO RELAX

Your enthusiasm for stimulating your child needs to be held in moderation. Do too much with her and she'll become exhausted, apathetic, and unresponsive. She benefits from having periods of relaxation on her own, choosing what she wants to do at that moment.

Make sure she has episodes on her own each day to play with toys and games of her own choice. Leisure time spent watching television, playing, or drawing without anyone giving her suggestions affords her an opportunity to make her own decisions. It also allows her time to reflect on the activities that occurred earlier in the day and to plan ahead. Your child doesn't need to be on the go the whole time.

Once she has had a break like this during the day, you'll find that she is well rested, full of enthusiasm, and ready for the next round of exciting stimulation activities that lie in store for her.

Above This little boy has taken time out from a group of children to play with a toy that interests him, a show of independence that will allow him to develop his skills in making his own decisions.

The Bilingual Child
Raising a Bilingual Child

Some parents speak a language at home that is different from the language used by the country in which they live; perhaps they are from another country and have not yet mastered the language of their new country, or perhaps they specifically want their child to learn the language of their former country.

The two most common strategies that parents choose for raising a bilingual child are to speak only the first language at home for the first three or four years and then allow the child to learn the second language when he starts playgroup or day care, or to speak both languages at home right from the start.

If you have the option of raising your child in a bilingual family home, you need to consider very carefully the most suitable technique for ensuring that your child's all-around language development is maximized. This has to be your top priority. Here are some key points for you to think about:

- **Confusion** You want to be sure that learning two languages at the same time during the early years won't result in your child becoming confused.
- **Rate of progress** Parents are often concerned by the fact that it is not possible for a child to learn two languages simultaneously and at the same rate at which he would learn only one.
- **Dominance** Even if you choose to speak both languages at home, you still need to decide which one will be used more frequently.
- **Delay** You may be worried that by teaching him only the minority language during the early years, your child will face an uphill struggle once he starts school and has to learn a new language.

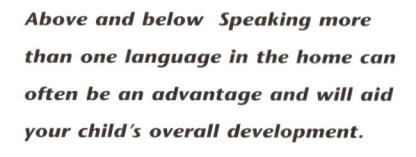

Above and below Speaking more than one language in the home can often be an advantage and will aid your child's overall development.

Above and left If your child's first language is different from the one used in the country where he lives, you will need to address any issues that may hamper his general language development.

PSYCHOLOGICAL STUDIES

Although there have been many different investigations into the way bilingual children develop mastery of language, there is no one "right" method that proves to be better than all the others. The fact is that some children seem to have problems with language development as a result of having to learn two languages at the same time during the early years, whereas other children appear to sail through this experience without any problem whatsoever.

Research findings do confirm, however, that if you choose to teach your child both languages at home from birth onward, you should expect his language development in both languages to be slower than that of his peers who learn only one language. You'll find that his vocabulary is smaller in each language, his sentences are shorter, and he uses fewer adjectives and pronouns compared with children the same age who are learning only one language at home. However, there is strong evidence that this difference soon evaporates once he starts going to school.

On the positive side, some studies have found that bilingualism before the age of 4 or 5 years actually improves a child's overall understanding of grammar later on, giving him an advantage over his peers. A child's understanding of meaning may also benefit from bilingualism. It's almost as if learning that there are at least two words for every object teaches him early on that the meanings of words are dynamic and complex.

MAKE YOUR CHOICE

It's entirely up to you to decide on the way you want to approach bilingualism in your home, based on your beliefs, personalities, and personal circumstances. You may, however, find it helpful to consider the following action plan:

1. Select the core language If you decide to use both languages from birth, select one language to speak exclusively for, say, the first six months. This gives your infant a grounding in these particular language sounds before hearing alternatives.

2. Introduce the second language After a few months, start to introduce elements of the second language indirectly, perhaps by letting him listen to songs or videos in that language. Do this gradually but consistently.

3. Give him time Your child needs time to grasp the concept that he hears two different language sounds at home. He slowly learns that each set of words belongs to a different language, though expect some crossover between the two.

4. Even things up When he is around 2 years old, speak both languages with the same frequency at home. Your child can switch between them with ease, and he recognizes that each one has its own characteristics and structures.

5. Take him to nursery school At the age of 2 or 3 years, enroll your child in day care or nursery school. You'll be surprised at how quickly he adapts and learns to use each language in its appropriate context.

6. Avoid confrontation Once your child is competent in each language, he'll choose the one that helps him best express his feelings at home. Don't insist that he always speak only one language, because this could create battles between you.

Special Needs
Children with Language Development Difficulties

A significant number of children have a pattern of speech and language development that does not follow the typical path. For instance, your baby might have a hearing difficulty that affects the rate at which she learns to speak, or she may have a visual difficulty that affects her ability to understand body language, or her learning skills may be weak, resulting in difficulties with her understanding of spoken language.

Always remember that a child with these sorts of problems has the same emotional needs as any other child—for love, care, and security—but special needs when it comes to learning effective communication.

Below Use brightly colored and textured toys to stimulate your child from an early age.

IDENTIFYING SPECIAL NEEDS

The key developmental difficulties that affect your child's grasp of spoken language and body language are problems with hearing, vision, and learning skills. These are often not immediately apparent at birth, becoming more obvious only later on. The information provided throughout this book indicates the approximate timing of each progressive step in your child's communication skills from birth through the age of 3 years.

Remember, however, that these are only guidelines and that there are wide individual differences. However, if you have any concerns about your child's progress in speech, language, and communication at any age, discuss them with your family doctor.

Parents often claim that their concerns about their child's speech development are rarely taken seriously by professionals. Many feel that they are dismissed with the explanation that they should "wait until she is older." Before visiting your doctor to discuss your worries about your infant's progress with language and communication, write a list of points that concern you with examples of what occurred. Specific points like these are more likely to be listened to than general concerns.

USE POSITIVE STRATEGIES

Language stimulation becomes even more important when your child has special needs, because she may not progress spontaneously from normal everyday experience alone. She probably requires more help with language than you'd typically expect for a child her age.

Take a positive approach in the way you encourage your child. Bear in mind that for every problem affecting speech and body language development, there are helpful practical strategies you can use.

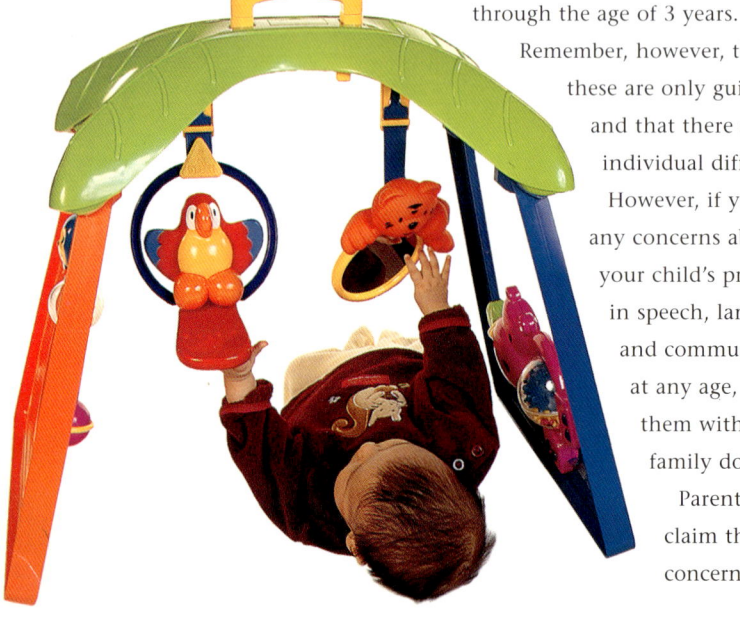

If your child can't hear very well:
- **Make sure** that she can see your face when you speak to her. Since her hearing is less sensitive, let her see your lips moving as you talk to her so that she can use visual cues instead of relying solely on auditory cues.
- **Encourage** her to wear hearing aids if they are prescribed for her. Hearing aids won't make her hearing perfect, but they will increase the volume and range of sounds she can hear.
- **Use toys** that are visually attractive and interesting to touch. Since the noises of, say, a rattle are dulled by her hearing difficulty, choose toys that are also bright and interesting to look at and that have varying textures on different surfaces.

If she has difficulty with her sight:
- **Find other ways** to enable her to access the information. Use brightly colored toys with a variety of textures, and move her hands over them so that she feels things when another child might just look at them.
- **Tell her** about all that is happening around her. Your very vivid descriptions of events encourage her language development almost as much as if she could see them herself.
- **Make best use** of lighting. There's no point, for example, in standing with your back to a bright sunlit window when you talk to your child, because she won't be able to make you out at all. Balance lighting to match her visual needs.

If she has difficulty with learning skills:
- **Accept** that she'll need more time to make progress with language. Moving from babbling to single words, and from single words to phrases, will take her longer. Her progress is slower than expected, so be patient.
- **Teach concepts** in small steps. For instance, some children quickly learn that the word "dog" applies to all animals in that category, not just to their own pet, but a child with learning difficulties might take longer to make that generalization.
- **Provide** lots of repetition. You may find that you need to explain the meaning of the same word over

Above Letting your children mix socially with other children will aid their general development and teach them how to interact.

and over again before she grasps it fully. Repetition helps her consolidate her understanding.

And if your child has a problem making speech sounds:
- **Accept advice** from a speech and language therapist. This professional gives parents guidance on exercises they can use with their child at home to improve the way she actually forms the words.
- **Listen to her talk** without interruption. She knows what she wants to say, but can't form the words clearly enough. It's important not to reduce her motivation for speech by making her repeat everything or by becoming frustrated.
- **Let her mix** with other children whose speech is fine. Of course, she may experience difficulties communicating with them, but this potential disadvantage is more than outweighed by the benefits of interacting with others.

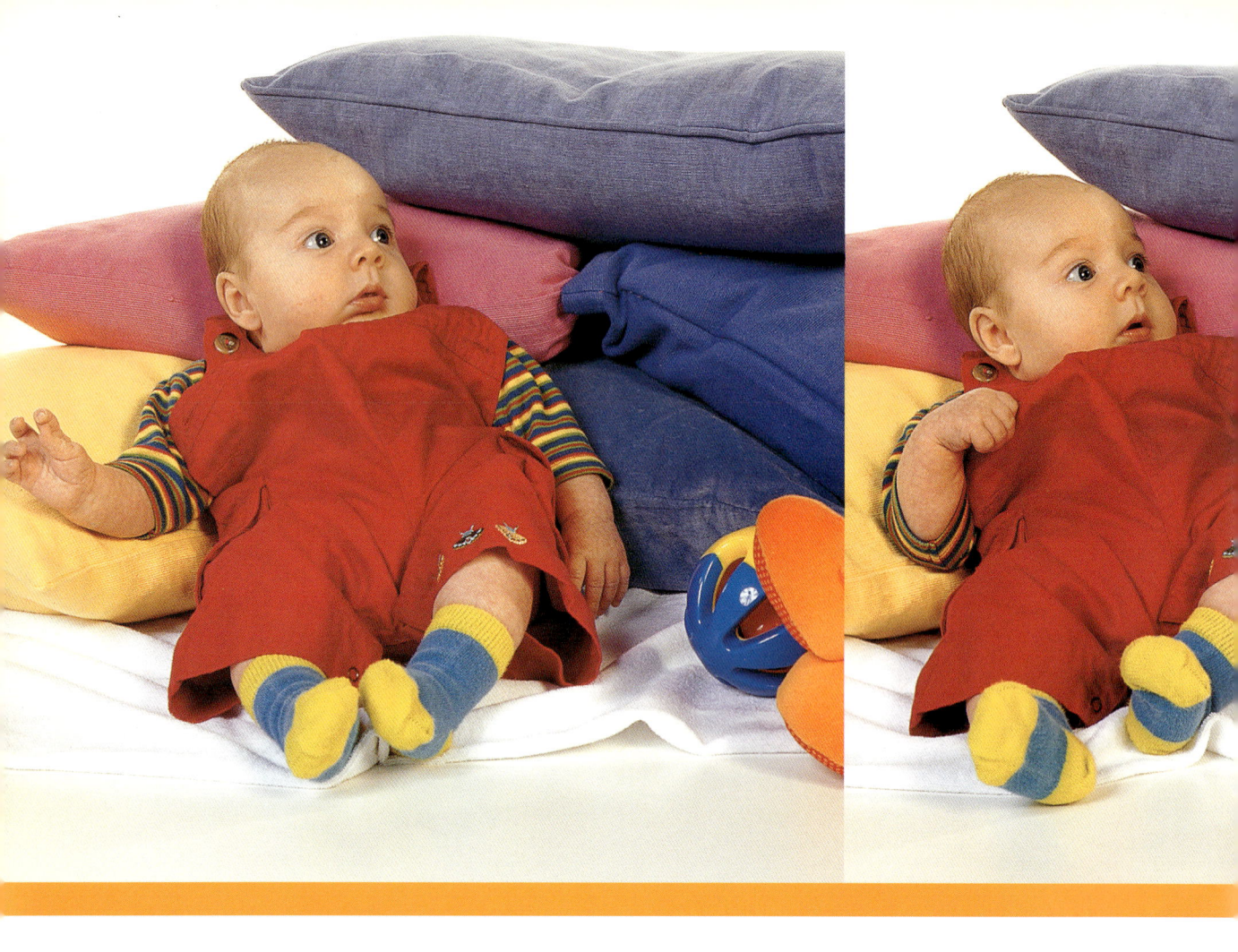

Birth–3 Months

What's amazing about your new baby is that although he can't talk, or even pronounce any individual vowels or consonants, he can communicate with you using sounds. For instance, your baby uses screams and cries to let you know that he is hungry, unhappy, or uncomfortable because his diaper is full. He also makes more gentle sounds to indicate to the world that he is relaxed and contented. And these sounds are combined with body, arm, and leg movements to convey even more meaning to you. You will soon get to know the meaning of his body language.

Language Development
Early Language Abilities

As your young baby lies in front of you on the changing mat or in her crib, she looks so vulnerable, so dependent. And she is. She needs your help, love, and support just to survive, never mind to progress. But your baby is not as powerless and unskilled as she appears. Psychological research has shown that a child's language skills are relatively advanced, even at this very early stage.

Aside from being able to generate sounds to attract your attention and express her feelings, here are some of the other communication abilities present in your baby when she is 3 months old or younger:

● **Consonant differentiation** Babies as young as 1 month react differently to different single consonant sounds. For instance, if the single sound "p" is repeatedly pronounced to her and then the single sound "b" is introduced, her heart rate alters at that point, indicating her awareness that there has been a change.

● **Vowel differentiation**
There is evidence that babies can spot the difference between vowel sounds, which can be harder to detect than consonant differences because vowels have greater similarity. (The difference between "a" and "e" is not as marked as between "t" and "z.")

● **Crying sensitivity**
A baby only a few hours old reacts differently to a human cry than she does to a computer-generated cry—she becomes more upset by the human sound of distress. This remarkable finding suggests that she is preprogrammed to react to human sounds.

Above *A newborn baby has limited vision, so make sure she can see your face when you talk to her by holding her close to you.*

● **Intonation awareness**
One study found that at the age of 4 or 5 days, a new baby distinguishes between words spoken to her in her own language and words spoken to her in a foreign language. This ability to differentiate is probably based on the different stresses and intonation of each language.

Left *From the very start most babies go through short periods in the day when they are contented and alert; this is when they will be most receptive and responsive.*

0–3 months

THE MAIN CHANGES TO LOOK FOR:

- **Birth** She announces her arrival into this world with a loud cry—that roar is just what she needs to get her lungs and vocal cords going! When hearing a loud noise, such as a door banging, she probably reacts by blinking her eyes or screwing up her nose and face.

- **1 week** Your baby stares closely at your face when you talk to her. You can't help but notice that her eyes are fixed on you when you say soothing words as you hold her close to you. It's as though she has an innate interest in the sounds of language, even though she can't make a huge range of sounds herself.

- **1 month** Different sorts of cries arise from different situations. For instance, your baby's cry when she is bored and wants attention is noticeably different from her cry when she is hungry. These variations in cries reflect the variations in her emotions and moods.

- **2 months** When you listen closely to the sounds that your baby makes now, you'll discover that they are not always the same—she probably makes at least two different vowel-like sounds. Of course, these are not like words and they are without any meaning, but their use reflects a significant change in her sound production system.

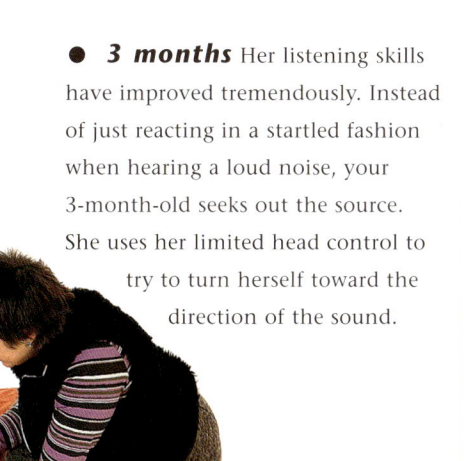

- **3 months** Her listening skills have improved tremendously. Instead of just reacting in a startled fashion when hearing a loud noise, your 3-month-old seeks out the source. She uses her limited head control to try to turn herself toward the direction of the sound.

Above This 2-month-old follows the movement of a noisy rattle with her eyes and touches it when it is brought close to her.

Language in the Womb

Studies have found that newborns prefer their mother's speech to the speech of strangers. The only way this connection could have been formed is through hearing the mother's speech while they were in the womb.

Another investigation taped pregnant women reading three different stories out loud. Then, one story was randomly picked and each mother-to-be read that "target" story out loud several times each day during the last couple of months of her pregnancy. When the babies were 2 or 3 days old, they listened to the three story tapes that their mothers had recorded at the start of the investigation. In virtually every instance, the baby reacted differently when hearing the target story than when hearing the other two.

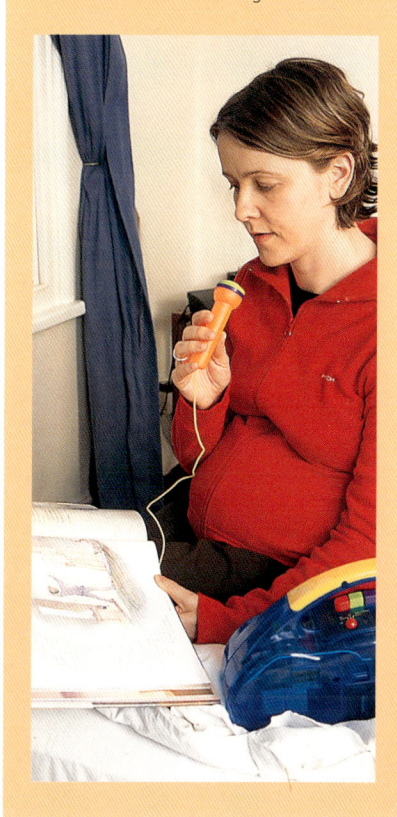

23

Body Language
I'm Talking to You

Your baby's lack of spoken language doesn't keep him from communicating with you—one method of nonverbal expression involves his use of body movements to let you know what he thinks and feels. Through actions using his arms and legs, facial expressions, and head movements, he is able to express some of his inner feelings to you. This nonverbal communication starts very early in his life.

Many of his early movements are automatic reflex actions. Take the startle reflex of the newborn, for instance, which lasts until around the end of the second or third month of life. This shows when he feels that he is about to be dropped. Similarly, there's the palmar grasp, when he instinctively wraps his hand around a finger placed in the palm of his hand. However, his arm and leg movements very gradually come under his control. This increasing mastery of his limb, trunk, and head movements means that, for example, you can recognize that he has a sore tummy when he draws his knees tightly up to his stomach, with his arms tense. Likewise, you can tell he is relaxed when he lies flat on his back, gazing wide-eyed at the musical mobile dangling within his line of vision. His nonverbal communication tells you a lot.

Facial expression is another way of conveying his emotions without words. Psychologists have identified seven basic facial expressions that adults are capable of generating. These are unhappiness, joy, surprise, interest, disgust, terror, and rage, and almost certainly you are able to identify the underlying feeling that is conveyed by any of these expressions when you see them on someone's face. Not only does your newborn baby have enough control over his facial muscles to create all of these facial expressions himself, but he makes them in appropriate circumstances. It's amazing to think he can convey so much to you without saying a word.

Below This baby's interest in the mobile is revealed by her intent facial expression and by movements of her arms and legs.

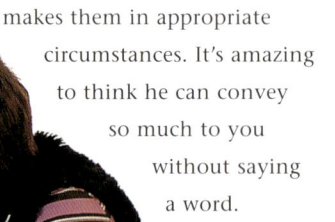

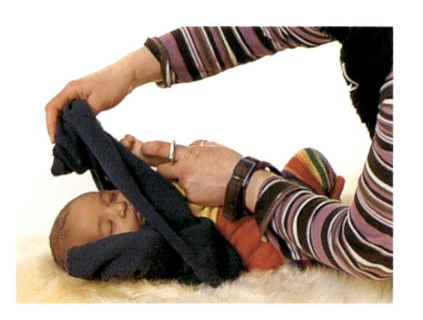

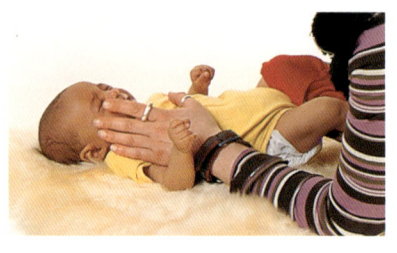

Above Many young babies object when their diaper is changed, but your touch and familiar voice will provide reassurance even though it may not stop the crying!

0–3 months

CRYING SPEAKS LOUDER THAN WORDS

Even just a couple of days after the birth, you'll already be aware that your baby has different cries to express his different moods and sensations. You will gradually develop an ability to tell one cry from another, enabling you to satisfy his different needs. This responsiveness to your baby's body language helps strengthen the emotional attachment between you, forming a close relationship.

Here are some of the typical cries you can expect to hear between birth and 3 months, their accompanying body movements, and their probable underlying meaning:

- **"It's feeding time"**
A cry from hunger is an automatic response in all babies. In most instances, this is one of those cries that starts off reasonably quiet, and then gets louder and louder. There are occasionally pauses for a few seconds as he swallows great gulps of air, but the crying is relentless.

- **"It's playing time"**
Your baby needs to be stimulated. True, he can amuse himself to some extent, but he really needs you to play with him, talk to him, and interact with him. When bored, he uses crying almost like a shout. It's not a distressed cry, just a loud noise to attract your attention.

- **"It's changing time"**
Your baby doesn't like to lie in a dirty diaper, and he wriggles his body about to let you know of his discomfort. His crying is not so sharp, because his distress is not so great. He may stop his tears occasionally, but will keep crying until given a new diaper.

Right This mother instinctively soothes her baby by holding her close so that she can see her face while she talks gently.

Imitation

Although your new baby has a wide range of facial expressions with which to communicate feelings without words, there is evidence from psychological research that he also has an ability to harmonize these with your own facial expressions in a reciprocal exchange.

In one study, for instance, each young baby was shown the face of an adult with his mouth open, an adult with his tongue stuck out, and an adult with his lower lip protruding—all facial movements that a new baby can make anyway. The researchers found that each baby very quickly began to imitate the adult facial expression, which suggests that he tried to interpret the other person's body language and made a sympathetic response of his own.

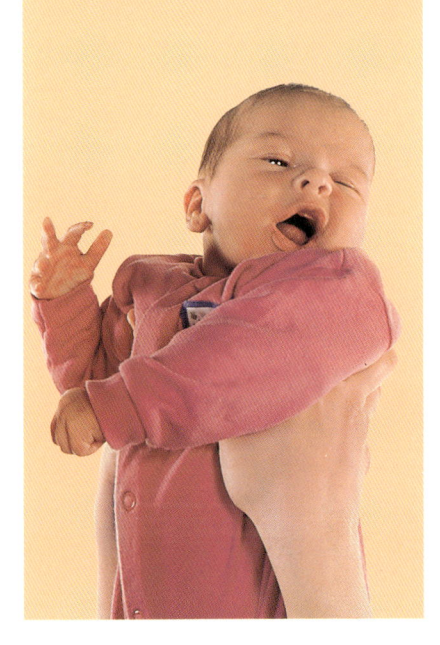

25

Top Tips to Help Your Child

Encourage Talking

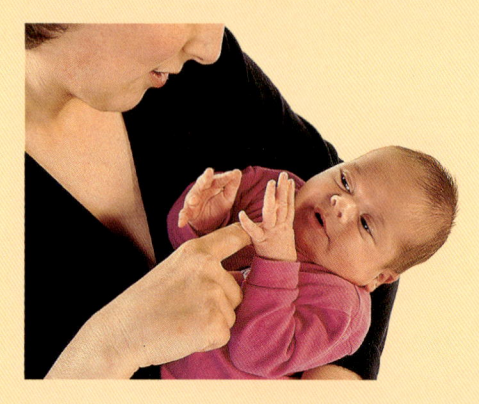

- **Talk to your baby** The fact that she doesn't understand a single word you say to her does not reduce the value of your spoken communication; her excited reaction confirms that she loves having you talk to her. Chat to her during feeding, changing, when taking her somewhere by car—indeed, when you are doing anything at all.

- **Vary your tone** You spontaneously use exaggerated tones, intonation, and facial expressions when speaking to your baby, in a way that you don't when talking to an older child or adult. Known as "parentese," this form of spoken language grabs your baby's interest in communication.

- **Use eye contact** She wants you to look at her firmly in the eye in a loving, smiling way when you speak to her. As a newborn baby, her vision naturally focuses on a point that is approximately 8–10 inches (20–25 cm) away from her face. So hold her face at that distance from your own when chatting to her.

- **Sing songs** There is one thing you can be sure of: no matter how awful other people may think your singing is, your baby just adores it! Hearing you sing nursery rhymes or lullabies stimulates her interest in language and makes her want to try to sing along with you. Let her see your face clearly while you are singing.

- **Respond to her sounds** By the age of 2 months your infant starts to make cooing sounds, which sound like words but actually have no meaning. However, chat back to her as though you are having a conversation, because this technique lets her become familiar with the concept of turn-taking in language.

- **Soothe her** After she has had a bath and is snug in her bedtime outfit, hold her securely on your lap and gently soothe her by slowly stroking her hair or the side of her cheek. Sing gently and softly to her at the same time. She loves this game, which helps her relax, and she listens to your words.

- **Talk to her about noises** As you take her on a trip outdoors, point out all the different sounds to your baby. Tell her, for example, that the chirping sounds are from a bird perched in the tree, that the sharp noise is a car sounding its horn, and that the rustling sound is the wind blowing through the leaves.

0 – 3 months

Use and Interpret Body Language

● **Check your interpretations** In addition to interpreting her cries, tell your baby what you think they mean. For instance, if you suspect she is crying from boredom, pick her up and say to her, "I can see you are bored, but now we are going to play." This can help to establish a link in her mind between spoken language and body language.

● **Make a response** React to her body language even though you are not exactly sure what she is trying to tell you. If what you do results in her calming down and relaxing, then you know you got it right the first time. And if it doesn't elicit the positive reaction you had hoped for, then just be prepared to try something else.

● **Use vivid facial expressions** Your baby responds best to you when your own body language is obvious rather than subtle. That's why she smiles more readily when your own smile is broad, not minimal—it is easier for her to understand. Remember that she learns from you and picks up mannerisms by observing you.

● **Reflect her feelings** Your baby is naturally sociable and she wants to share her feelings with you; she has an instinctive need to do this. That's why her laughter intensifies when you show your own obvious delight at her happiness—she chuckles even more loudly. Try to "mirror" her positive feelings in this way.

● **Play tickling games** Once she is a few weeks old, you'll discover that she responds to gentle tickling. At first she squirms as though in discomfort, but by the age of 3 months tickling makes her chuckle with delight. Run your fingers softly up and down her sides, or tickle the soles of her feet and watch her giggle.

● **Take crying seriously** No baby cries "just for the sake of it" or simply to annoy her parents. There is always a reason for her tears. No matter how fed up you may be with yet another bout of crying or screaming, she is trying to tell you something. Do your best to find out what troubles her.

● **Sing action songs** During the day, make a point of singing songs to her that involve gentle, controlled actions. For instance, rocking her in your arms while singing "Rock-a-bye-baby" makes the whole experience more vivid for her. Be careful, though, not to make the actions too vigorous.

Toys Selection of rattles that make varied sounds ● mobile for above the crib ● toys that make a noise when activated or moved ● baby picture book ● brightly colored toys that attach to the side of the crib ● large plastic ring ● handheld music box ● selection of small toys of varying sizes and textures

27

Questions and Answers

Q I feel silly talking to my baby all the time. The fact that she can't talk back and can't even understand what I'm saying to her makes me feel foolish. What should I do?

A Talk to her anyway—it's as simple as that. You may feel embarrassed prattling away to a baby who can't talk back, but reassure yourself that your use of language is good for her. Remember that she absolutely adores you and is fascinated by everything you do. When you talk to her and she listens to the wide range of different sounds that you produce, she learns from that and eventually starts to imitate them herself. That's not silliness—that is good old-fashioned language stimulation and it only does her good.

Q I just don't seem to be able to learn the different meanings of my baby's cries. All the other mothers are better than me at this. What am I doing wrong?

A You are doing absolutely nothing wrong. It just seems that everybody else knows what their baby wants, when in fact they are as uncertain as you. So have a bit more confidence in yourself. The only way to gain a more accurate interpretation of your baby's cries is by using trial and error. In other words, make an effort to soothe him and see what happens. Sometimes you'll have success and other times it will take you several attempts before your baby settles. This is the normal learning process that all parents go through.

Q At what age should a baby show her first smile? My friend's baby smiled when he was only a couple of days old and yet mine is now 4 weeks and hasn't smiled at all.

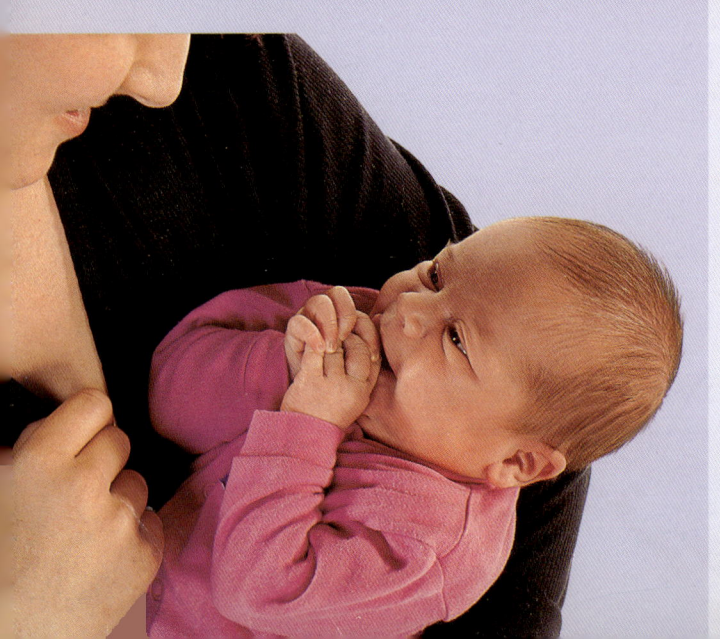

A Babies typically show their first genuine smile around the age of 5 or 6 weeks, though it really does vary from baby to baby. It is highly unlikely that your friend's baby actually smiled within a couple of days of the birth. Almost certainly what you saw was a facial expression that resembled a smile, but that simply served the purpose of enabling him to release gas from his mouth! Continue to play with your baby and you'll find that her first smile magically appears in the next couple of weeks.

0 – 3 months

Q Is it sensible to use "baby talk" with my infant aged 2 months? I notice that many people use words with him such as "choo choo" instead of "train" and "bow wow" instead of "dog." Should I encourage this?

A It's really up to you to decide on this one. Some people argue that there is no point in teaching a baby a word such as "bunny," because he will eventually have to replace it with the proper word "rabbit." Others, however, support the use of baby talk on the grounds that it is easier for an infant to understand and subsequently use, and is therefore a good stepping-stone in language progress. Either way, your occasional use of baby talk won't do him any harm.

Q Someone told me that television is bad for my 3-month-old baby, and that it will harm his development because it will discourage him from speaking. Is that right?

A The situation is not so clear-cut. Of course a baby who is left in front of the television for long periods instead of receiving stimulation from his parent may become bored, listless, and less likely to vocalize. But that's a very extreme state that you are unlikely to allow. Sporadic, short episodes of television-watching at this age can actually stimulate your baby's language development, because they provide him with a vast array of sights, sounds, and forms of language. Your baby will benefit from watching television if it is part of a balanced program of language stimulation opportunities.

Q I'm worried that my baby doesn't make a lot of sounds. He is 1 month old and yet is happy to lie quietly in his crib. It's not that he is silent, more that he isn't very vocal. Should I be concerned?

A Every baby is a unique individual with his own characteristics. In the same way that some adults are more talkative than others, some babies are more vocal than others. What matters is that your baby is making a range of sounds in different situations, which is convincing evidence that his expected early language skills are present. Your worry is really about the quantity of his vocalizations, not about their quality. This is probably a reflection of his personality, nothing more, and is not an indication of an underlying language problem.

29

Development

1 Week Skills

MOVEMENT
- Sucks in reflex when a soft object is placed in her mouth.
- Automatically swallows milk on her tongue.
- If startled she will arch her back and throw her arms and legs in the air (Moro reflex).
- Moves legs in a reflex stepping action if her feet are lowered onto a flat surface.
- When her cheek is stroked she turns her head to find the nipple ("rooting" reflex).
- Cannot hold her head without support or raise it from the mattress.
- While sleeping she often lies with arms and legs in the fetal position.

HAND–EYE COORDINATION
- Grasps items placed in her hand in a reflex reaction but is unable to hold on.
- Focuses on an object that is roughly 8–10 inches (20–25 cm) from her face.
- Often holds her hand in a fist.
- Blinks in reflex when an object approaches her face quickly.

LANGUAGE
- Tries to look at you when you speak.
- Reacts to sudden noises.
- Recognizes her parents' voices and can distinguish high and low pitches.
- Makes eye contact.

1 Month Skills

MOVEMENT
- Can raise her head a couple of inches when lying facedown.
- Moves her head from side to side but mostly lies with her right cheek on the mattress.
- Kicks her arms and legs in the air.
- Screws up her face when she experiences a bitter taste.
- Tries to turn onto her side when lying on her back.
- When startled will still arch her back and fling out her arms and legs in the Moro reflex action.

HAND–EYE COORDINATION
- Stares at objects about 8–10 inches (20–25 cm) from her face.
- Will follow objects that are moved a few inches from side to side.
- Moves her hands without control but can move her fist to her mouth.
- May pull her blanket toward her.
- The grasp reflex is still strong when something is placed in her palm.

LANGUAGE
- Uses a wider range of cries; parents begin to distinguish between cries of hunger, boredom, tiredness, discomfort.
- Conveys mood by agitated arm and leg movements, and facial expressions such as mouth twitching or staring.

2 Month Skills

MOVEMENT
- Limited control over arms and legs.
- Holds a small object for a few moments.
- Holds her head off the mattress for a couple of seconds.
- Neck control increases and is beginning to support the weight of her head when she is carried.
- Early reflexes (Moro, grasp reflex) are fading.

HAND–EYE COORDINATION
- Hand control begins; her hands are mostly open with fingers becoming more flexible.
- Peers with interest at her fingers.
- The grasp reflex fades.
- Will close her fingers around a small object placed in her palm and move the object toward her face.
- Tries but cannot reach accurately for a small toy.

LANGUAGE
- Makes a cooing, repetitive vowel sound when relaxed.
- Uses a couple of identifiable but meaningless sounds.
- Becomes quiet when she is lifted up.
- Moves her eyes to look for the source of a noise.
- Watches the gestures and body language of those talking to her.
- Is encouraged to repeat sounds when

3 Month Skills

MOVEMENT
- Improved head control means she can hold her head off the mattress for longer whether lying on her tummy or back.
- Enjoys being held upright, and head and neck movements become more varied.
- Leg movements become quite vigorous when kicking.
- Better at moving her body around her crib.

HAND–EYE COORDINATION
- Watches an object as it moves around the room.
- Stretches out her hand toward an object close to her.
- Grabs a toy when placed in her hand.
- Thrusts her hands toward source of food.
- Will stare at pictures in books and try to touch them.
- Peers at objects and tries to put them in her mouth to explore their properties.

LANGUAGE
- More attentive to distinctive sounds she hears.
- Listening skills have improved and she becomes quiet when she hears a small noise.
- Enjoys hearing you sing to her.
- Gurgles and coos in response to sounds; will gurgle to herself for several minutes.
- Makes at least two distinct sounds such as "oooh" and "aaah."

0 – 3 months

LEARNING
- Can focus her attention on you.
- Can distinguish the faces of her parents from those of strangers.
- Can recognize her parents' scent within days.
- Is sensitive to touch and is calmed by being held.
- Has varying periods of alertness but sleeps 80 percent of the day in about eight naps.

SOCIAL AND EMOTIONAL
- Enjoys your company and responds positively to your voice.
- Stares at your face when it is within 8–10 inches (20–25 cm) of hers.
- Cries when she is unhappy or uncomfortable.
- Moves her arms and legs about in excitement.

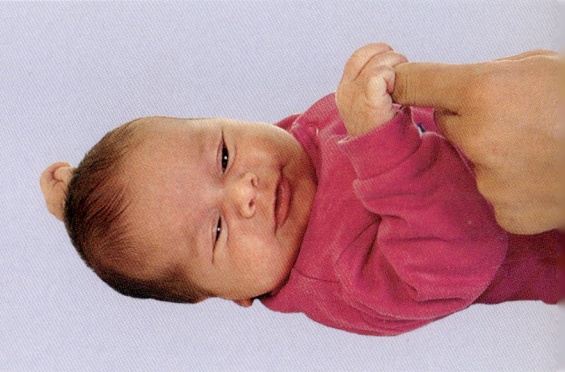

- Makes sounds when she is happy.
- Responds positively to soothing words.

LEARNING
- Loves to look at her surroundings.
- Will stare for longer at blue and green objects than red ones.
- Is fascinated by objects placed nearby.
- Will remember an object that reappears within a few seconds of moving.

SOCIAL AND EMOTIONAL
- Enjoys a cuddle and being smiled at.
- Responds positively when you talk and sing to her.
- Makes eye contact.
- Is able to relax at bathtime, kicking and splashing in the water.
- Cries from hunger, boredom, tiredness, discomfort.
- May mimic if you stick your tongue out at her.

- Begins to recognize your voice as distinct from others.
- Is alert for about one in every ten hours.

---

people smile and talk back to her.

LEARNING
- Can control vision more accurately and peers at an object moved in a pattern in front of her.
- Likes listening to music and is comforted by background sounds such as the washing machine or car engine.
- Becomes excited in anticipation, for example when she sees the bath.
- Begins to coordinate her senses by looking toward sounds.
- Clearly distinguishes between people, voices, tastes.

SOCIAL AND EMOTIONAL
- Has shown you her first smile and is likely to smile if you beam at her.
- Enjoys attention from you and others.
- Stays awake for longer if people interact with her.
- May begin to sleep through the night.
- Begins to amuse herself when left alone by looking around, tracking, and batting at objects.
- Feeding becomes a social experience: she looks at you while you feed and talk to her.

LEARNING
- Sees a link between her hand movement and the toy's reaction; a toy might rattle when she moves it.
- Improved memory allows her to anticipate events such as feeding, and reappearance of a person playing peek-a-boo.
- Recognizes familiar music.
- Will imitate actions such as opening and closing her mouth, sticking out her tongue.
- Fascinated by her hands, which she fans in front of her face.
- Begins to differentiate family members by sight and the sounds of their voice.
- Can tell the difference between a woman's face and a man's face.

SOCIAL AND EMOTIONAL
- More responsive to any adult who shows interest in her.
- Thrives on attention, even tries to attract attention when a parent is near her.
- Has a broad range of facial expressions to express her moods.
- Smiles a lot more readily, and her crying decreases.

4–6 Months

Whereas until now your baby made only "cooing" sounds that had no meaning whatsoever, during this period he moves into the "babbling" phase. His maturing vocal cords enable him to make a broader range of sounds. You'll find that he tends to make these same sounds both when he is with you and when left on his own in his crib. Babbling is the first major indication that your baby has begun to use spoken language to communicate with you. Increased control over head, body, leg, and arm movements at this age also allows him to bring nonverbal communication under more control.

Language Development
Babbling

The babbling that you hear from your growing baby as she approaches her sixth month consists of distinctive sounds that are clearly recognizable as individual syllables. Most psychologists agree that a baby's first words—which don't appear until later—are based on these small units of babbled speech.

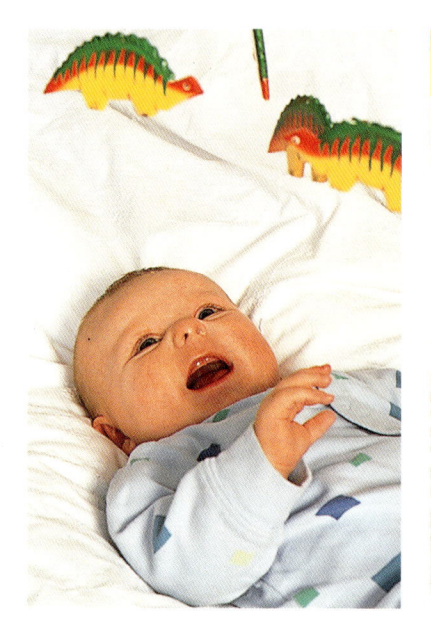

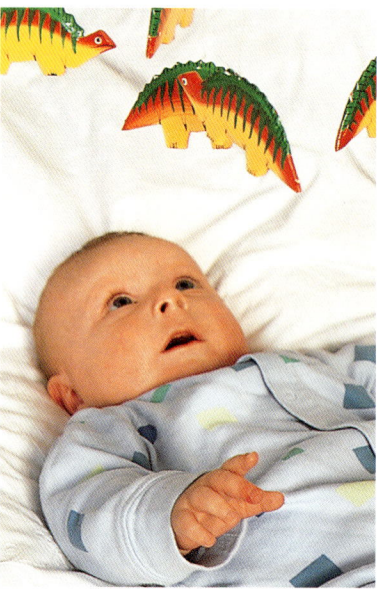

This is coupled with changes in listening and attention skills. Studies have found that at this age a baby's rate and quantity of vocalizations actually decrease compared with the previous months when her parent talks to her. That is thought to be caused by her improving listening skills as your baby pays more attention to what you say.

Researchers have also found that babbling causes parents spontaneously to teach their infant conversational skills. What happens is that the baby's vocal responsiveness between 4 and 6 months acts as positive feedback, which stimulates her parent's vocalizations. The parent or caregiver assumes that the baby has genuine meaning underlying her language sounds (even though that might not be accurate), and so starts to talk to her using a more traditional style of conversation in which the baby babbles, the parent speaks, and the baby then babbles again, each taking turns to contribute to this "dialogue." This is an instinctive way in which parents give their babies lessons in social conversation.

Of course, at this age your baby perceives more complex sounds than she makes, and her sound differentiation skills are probably better than you think. Whereas a very young baby can distinguish between two consonant sounds that are presented alone, she can now pick out different sounds from

Above By this age your baby's interest in something he sees will be apparent in his facial expression and in the way he strains his arms and upper body to reach it.

consonant-vowel combinations. For example, one study of 4-month-old babies found that they became bored and disinterested (as assessed by their rate of sucking) when the same two consonant-vowel sounds were repeated, such as "baa" and "baa." But when one aspect of these consonant-vowel units was subtly changed, for example to "baa" and "paa," their rate of sucking noticeably increased, indicating that they can discriminate clearly between these two sound combinations.

4 – 6 months

THE MAIN CHANGES TO LOOK FOR:

● **4 months** By now she chuckles gleefully at anything that amuses her. You'll find that letting her glance at her own image reflected in a mirror brings squeals of delight. Tickling her brings a similar response, and your smile in return encourages her to use laughter as a way of communicating her happiness. Your infant is also a more attentive listener and turns her head more accurately to one side or the other when trying to detect where the noise is coming from—you'll see her strain her head when, out of her line of vision, you switch on her favorite music box.

● **5 months** Her sounds are more varied and more consistent than they were before, which is due partly to the development of the muscles and vocal cords associated with speech and partly to her general maturation. Your baby uses perhaps three or four different babbling sounds consistently, such as "b" or "m" or "w," though not in the same order, and you hear her use them again the next day. Sometimes she combines them to form larger strings such as "babababababa." It's almost as if she is thoroughly taken by her own ability to make these noises.

● **6 months** She loves listening to music, and her arms and legs move excitedly when her favorite tune is played. Sometimes gentle soothing music can be useful in helping her fall asleep. Although your infant continues to babble, you begin to get the impression that she's actually trying to talk to you—that there is some underlying meaning behind her babbling sounds. In particular, she's more tuned in to the social nature of language; she babbles, then pauses while you reply, then babbles.

Left At 4 months or so babies start to find their reflection in a mirror a source of immense fascination, and it will hold their attention for some time.

Understanding Meaning

One of the difficulties in knowing how much your infant actually understands of what you say to her is that she can't tell you—that would make things so much easier! The only way to assess her ability to understand meaning is by observing her behavior.

Between the fourth and sixth months, most children begin to develop awareness that their name refers to them. Talk to your friend while your baby sits comfortably in her baby chair, playing with a toy. When she's engrossed in the play, insert her name into one of your sentences. Don't pause artificially or make a special emphasis when you say it. You may find that she pauses, smiles, and looks at you, although many children don't fully recognize their name until months later.

Body Language
Movement Improves

Improvements in your child's physical development provide him with a greater ability to express himself nonverbally. For instance, when lying facedown on the mattress he can push his shoulders and head off the floor. That movement, combined with the wide-eyed expression on his face, tells you that he's bursting to connect with you. It's his way of saying, "Hello there. I want you to talk to me."

Left Once your baby can lift and keep his head and shoulders off the floor, it opens up a new way for him to view and explore.

Eye movements become part of his body language repertoire, especially now that he has more control over them. You know exactly what he means when he stares desperately at the bottle you are preparing, babbles angrily, and starts to cry. When he grabs a toy and bangs it loudly against the side of his crib, he could just be playing. However, his furrowed expression and fiery eyes let you know that on this occasion he is driven by temper, not playfulness.

Whereas before, crying was your infant's main means of nonverbal communication, which he used many times throughout the day (and night), tears and screams are relatively less frequent now. And when he does cry, there is usually a very specific reason, rather than simply general discomfort arising from hunger, thirst, or pain. Crying becomes more finely tuned in this sense, so it becomes easier for you to tell what his cries mean. You may find, for instance, that he suddenly starts to howl when someone talks to him while you push him around the supermarket. You know right away that he is anxious and wants a reassuring cuddle from you.

Below By 5 months or so your baby's curiosity knows no bounds, and with increasing agility he will explore anything he can reach with his hands and mouth.

4 – 6 months

SAYING NOTHING

Your infant is able to express a much wider range of feelings and ideas nonverbally. Other typical emotions expressed using body language at this age include

● **Rejection** At around 6 months when he sits upright in his high chair, he has no difficulty expressing his preference or dislike for any food that is presented to him. He may have a smile on his face when his hands push the bowl away, or when he turns his face to the side as you raise the spoon to his lips. Initially you could think he is just playing, but you soon realize that he's telling you, "I don't like this and I want something else in its place."

● **Curiosity** His desire to discover knows no limits. At this age, however, he is better able to express his inquisitiveness through the use of body language. Your attention is attracted by the strange noise emanating from his crib, and when you arrive there you can see him straining to get hold of something that is just outside his reach. The combination of his effort-induced groans and his stretching movements demonstrates that his actions are motivated by curiosity.

Above If your baby is unresponsive it may simply mean he is tired, but uncharacteristic listlessness can signal illness.

● **Ill-health** Lethargic body movements can carry as much meaning as active gestures. If your infant is normally on the go the whole time, full of enthusiasm during his waking hours, then any change toward listlessness should send a clear message to you. He could simply be tired and be about to fall asleep. More likely, however, he's indicating to you, "I don't feel well and I haven't got enough energy to play actively right now."

Left As soon as babies can sit up they will instinctively move their bodies forward to grasp objects that are out of reach—a preliminary step toward crawling.

Facial Emotions

The type and frequency of emotions conveyed through facial expression changes with age. In one study, psychologists studied dozens of face-to-face interactions between mothers and their babies, who were either 2 months old or 5 months old. The researchers noted the variety of facial expressions used by the babies at each age and then classified them according to the emotions they were judged to represent. Detailed analysis of the results showed that the most frequent emotion conveyed nonverbally by the babies aged 5 months was happiness. The next most frequent emotion was displeasure, and the third most frequent was interest. This was compared with babies aged 2 months, whose facial expressions conveyed (in descending order of frequency) displeasure, happiness, and interest.

37

Top Tips to Help Your Child

Encourage Talking

- **Show pleasure** Although your infant's innate desire to communicate with you continues unabated, her progress and interest in spoken language remain dependent on your approval and stimulation. One of the best forms of encouragement you can give her is to look enthusiastically at her when she babbles at you.

- **Pause in conversations** Remember that your infant needs time to understand the social rules of communication, to grasp that exchanging thoughts through the spoken word is a reciprocal arrangement involving both talking and listening. Allow gaps that are long enough for your infant to babble a response to you.

- **Pose questions** Of course she is not able to give a coherent reply to the sorts of questions you ask her, such as "Do you feel more comfortable now that I've changed your diaper?" Yet there is no harm in looking as though you expect her to answer you. Through this she is able to learn about the significance of accent and tone.

- **Play listening games** While she sits on the floor or lies in her crib playing quite contentedly, take a small bell and gently ring it from one corner of the room. Watch to see her reaction. Then ring it from other points in the room when she's not looking at you. This is a good way to sharpen her attention skills.

- **Read stories to her** It really doesn't matter what story you read, as long as it is written for a young audience. You can sit your infant firmly on your knee as you read to her, or you can position her so that she sits facing you. If you find that her attention wanders while you read, gently draw her interest back to the story.

- **Play different music** Sometimes she prefers to listen to a gentle lullaby, whereas at other times she prefers to hear more active music. Try to play a range of music for her, so that she hears different musical instruments and tunes played at various speeds and volumes. The more variety of musical sounds she hears, the better.

- **Encourage environmental awareness** Remember that your infant observes everything around her with great curiosity and interest. She wants you to help her understand by explaining things to her. So when you are outdoors with her, chat to her about the people and objects that you both see. She loves this.

4 – 6 months

Use and Interpret Body Language

● **Point to pictures** Your use of gestures to point to various pictures in a book while reading a simple story to her serves a number of purposes. It helps to maintain her interest and attention, reduces distractions, and enables her to understand that body movement can be a good way to communicate intention.

● **Recite action rhymes** She wants to get involved with you. Reciting a poem that includes actions makes the experience much more vivid for her and heightens her awareness of movement as part of communication. The rhyme about "This little piggy," which ends up with a tickle, will delight your infant.

● **Use facial expressions to make her giggle** The chances are that she will be thoroughly amused by some of the unusual facial expressions that you make, especially when they are accompanied by your calm voice. Although this is only a bit of fun, it once again demonstrates another aspect of body language to her.

● **Form connections between actions and outcomes** React to her negative nonverbal messages. For instance, if she pushes her food away and deliberately turns her plate over on the table, tell her not to do that; and if she throws a toy on the floor in temper, gently point out to her that this behavior is not acceptable.

● **Encourage water play** Bathtime is an ideal opportunity for your baby to use actions to express her emotions. Moving her arms, legs, feet, and hands excitedly in the water results in an instant splash. If she lacks confidence in the bath, make sure you hold her firmly along her back and under one arm so that she doesn't slip, and never leave your child unattended.

● **Give plenty of hugs** Close physical contact of a loving nature is one of the most basic ways in which you can tell your baby that you love her. Without you having to say a word, she realizes right away what a cuddle means—and she loves it. She responds nonverbally, too, by pressing her body close to yours.

● **Provide behavioral prompts** Your infant wants to discover more about the world around her, but there are times when she isn't sure what to do. At these times, you can model the appropriate behavior. For example, if you know she wants to find a toy but doesn't know how to do this, let her see you search for something.

Toys Plastic storybooks with large pictures ● cassette tapes with a wide range of children's songs ● story tapes ● lots of noisy toys with bells and rattles ● large play mat with animal or shape patterns ● bundle of wooden cubes ● baby gym that hangs over her as she lies on the floor ● crib activity center ● set of plastic nesting cups

39

Questions and Answers

Q Is it really possible that my 6-month-old baby can tell my voice apart from other people's voices that he hears?

A Yes. In fact he probably recognizes your voice long before that. If you think back to earlier times when you saw his face break into a large smile as you spoke to your baby while approaching him, you'll realize that initial voice recognition was present when he was much younger. However, his ability not only to identify your voice instantly but also to differentiate it from others he hears at the same time—for instance, when a group of relatives visit your house—steadily improves, too. So by the age of 6 months he has little difficulty identifying your voice from among all the others.

Q Why does my baby frown most of the time? People say he looks really grumpy when they see him, but he's actually very happy most days.

A This illustrates why you can't always gain an accurate interpretation of facial expression unless you know the infant's personality. Since parenting experience has told you that he's generally a happy, contented child, then you know that his frowns—normally associated with bad temper—don't indicate irritation. A more likely explanation is that his creased forehead is a sign of interest and concentration, and is simply his way of focusing his attention. You'll find that his use of this expression passes, and that as he matures and his other facial muscles become stronger, his furrowed brow appears less frequently.

Q My baby is 4 months old but still cries heavily for an hour each evening. Nothing I do calms him. My doctor says this is colic. What does this mean?

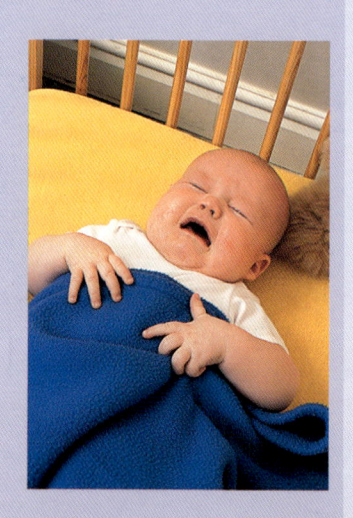

A "Colic" is the term used by some professionals to describe this particular form of crying. The baby is assumed to be experiencing a form of painful muscle spasm in his tummy that causes such distress. However, there is no scientific evidence to support the existence of colic. On the other hand, psychologists do not claim to understand the meaning of this cry, although some maintain that it is a baby's way of saying he wants to be the center of attention. Whatever the real explanation, you'll find that these dreadful evening bouts of crying soon cease.

4 – 6 months

Q Why doesn't my 4-month-old baby recognize his name when I say it? It's as though he really doesn't know I'm referring to him.

A Bear in mind that children make progress with their understanding of language at different rates, which means that although some babies recognize their own name by the time they are 4 months old, others do not. You can help your baby develop name awareness by using it more in your conversations with him: for instance, when you play with him say his name lots of times, and when you tell him that you are bringing one of his toys put his name in that, too. It's through language stimulation of this sort that he advances his grasp of language.

Q My baby loves bathtime and becomes excited when I start to undress him. But he now becomes excited when I open the cupboard to get the bath towel out, even before I undress him. Could he really know that this is the start of the process?

A His body language—those vigorous arm and leg movements—is clearly telling you, "I'm excited because in a moment you'll put me in the bath." This is a sign of his increased ability to see connections between events. He may be young, but he has already observed that preparation for bathtime doesn't just start with you undressing him, that there are earlier steps than this, such as getting the towel out of the cupboard. Hence, his body language conveys excitement.

Q I've noticed that my infant often becomes startled when I appear in front of his crib, even though I have spoken to him while approaching. Why is he so surprised by my arrival?

A He may not have perfectly clear hearing at the moment. A baby typically uses a number of cues to prepare for someone who is about to enter his line of vision—the sounds of that person's footsteps and of their voice are good indicators of an impending arrival. One of the possible explanations for your baby's behavior is that he doesn't hear these sounds very clearly—hence his total surprise when, from his point of view, you suddenly appear in front of him. Arrange an appointment to have his hearing checked.

41

Development

4 Month Skills

MOVEMENT
- Sits in an upright position with support.
- Turns from left side to right, and vice versa, without help.
- May start to roll over from front to back and vice versa.
- Pulls herself around the crib.
- Head doesn't flop around when you hold her.
- She can turn and move her head in all directions.
- Grasping is deliberate and is no longer just a reflex.

HAND–EYE COORDINATION
- Reaches out when you place her in the bath and slaps her hand in the water.
- Tries to grab objects near her.
- Stares at the place from which an object has dropped.
- Waves small toys held in her hand.
- Her eyesight has improved and she can focus on near and distant objects as well as an adult can.

LANGUAGE
- She gives a definite laugh when something entertains or amuses her.
- Makes vocalizations to attract your attention.
- Listens keenly to distinct noises.
- Shows pleasure through excited movement and delighted facial expressions.

LEARNING
- Recalls how to play with a familiar toy in a particular way.
- Peers at her own reflection in a mirror.
- Looks curiously at objects.

5 Month Skills

MOVEMENT
- Pushes her feet firmly against surfaces, such as the bottom of the crib.
- Moves around the floor by rolling and turning her body.
- Can keep her legs in the air and kick them about freely.
- Holds her head confidently when she is supported in an upright position.

HAND–EYE COORDINATION
- Watches you as you move around the room.
- Starts to look for an object that has slipped from her grasp.
- Lifts her hand toward a nearby object and reaches for it more accurately than she did before.
- Can hold a small toy in her hand.
- Has a firm grip and doesn't like to let go.

LANGUAGE
- Makes an increased range of sounds with consonants such as "w," "m," "b."
- Uses three or four babbling sounds at

6 Month Skills

MOVEMENT
- Sits up on her own without requiring any support.
- Pushes her head, chest, and shoulders off the floor when facedown.
- Shows first signs of crawling by drawing one knee to her tummy.
- Makes energetic body movements to try to propel herself along the floor.
- Becoming more adept at rolling from front to back and back to front.
- Twists and turns in all directions.

HAND–EYE COORDINATION
- Uses both hands in synchrony and can pass objects from one hand to the other.
- Keeps watching a toy that falls from her grip.
- Plays with toys more purposefully instead of just mouthing them.
- Enjoys dropping a toy and picking it up again repeatedly.
- Tries to feed herself by putting food to her mouth with her fingers.
- Grabs hold of the bottle or spoon while having her meal.

4 – 6 months

- May take two or three naps a day, and can be alert for up to an hour at a time.

SOCIAL AND EMOTIONAL
- Uses facial expressions to keep your attention.
- Chuckles spontaneously when she is feeling happy.
- Enjoys familiar situations such as feeding, bathing, dressing.
- Laughs loudly when she is tickled.
- Relaxes when you sing gently to her.

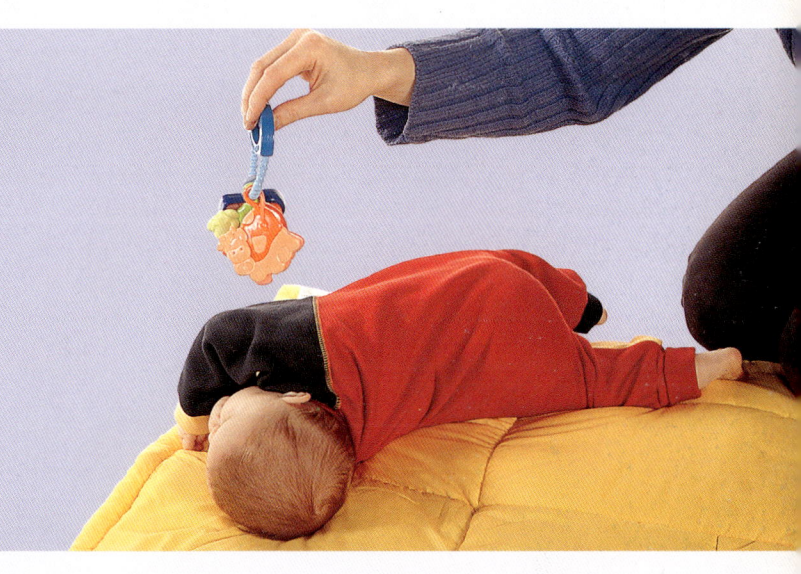

random, combining vowels and consonants; for example, "nanana."
- Vocalizes when you talk to her and may babble to you during gaps in your speaking.
- Imitates your facial expressions and observes your reaction to her.
- Tries to imitate sounds she hears.
- Listens intently and can hear almost as well as an adult.

LEARNING
- Likes to explore whenever she has the opportunity.
- Focuses well but prefers to look at objects within 3 feet (1m) of her.
- Is curious enough to handle any object close to her.
- Detects a sound source accurately by turning toward it.
- Drops one object when another attracts her interest.
- Weaning begins with the introduction of solid foods.

SOCIAL AND EMOTIONAL
- May form an attachment to a cuddly toy or other comforter and likes to have this object close to her when she goes to sleep.
- Can play on her own for short periods.
- Shows interest in new surroundings.
- Complains when you try to remove a toy from her hand.
- Can be shy when she is in the company of strangers.
- Smiles and vocalizes to attract attention.

LANGUAGE
- Synchronizes her speech with yours as though in conversation.
- Produces more different vowel and consonant sounds, for example, "f," "v," "ka," "da," "ma."
- Laughs when happy and now screams when angry.
- Makes gurgling noises when playing contentedly.
- Begins to react to the mood of music that she hears.

LEARNING
- Recognizes herself in a photograph or in a mirror.
- Switches her stare from one object to another as though comparing them.
- Holds a toy in each hand without dropping them.
- Actively reaches out for toys that attract her curiosity.
- May start to understand the meaning of the word "no."
- Can differentiate between men and women by their voice tones.

SOCIAL AND EMOTIONAL
- May become anxious in strange company and begin to cry.
- Chuckles in anticipation when you come toward her.
- Playfully holds on to a toy when you try to remove it.
- Coos or stops crying in response to familiar music.
- Turns when she hears her own name.
- Becomes anxious in some situations, for example when she has maneuvered herself into an awkward position.

43

7–9 Months

A more consistent pattern now develops in your infant's vocalizations. The random babbling of a few months ago is replaced by more controlled use of sounds—and he tends to use the same pattern of sounds in the same context. This change in the way he babbles indicates that meaning and purpose is beginning to emerge in his vocalizations. In addition, your infant starts to use varied sound combinations, joining two different consonant-vowel combinations in one utterance.
His body language during this period reflects the changes that occur in his desire for independence, his intention to be more sociable, and his increasing frustration.

Language Development
Representation

Language is not simply a series of random, meaningless sounds. Genuine language uses these sounds to represent, for instance, objects and people that may not even be directly in front of the speaker. So your infant's gradual development of language is connected to her increasing ability to understand representation—that is, her ability to think about objects and people she has seen previously.

This link between language, perception, and representation has led psychologists to study "object permanence"—a child's ability to realize an object still exists even though she may not actually see it at the time. After all, if she can't hold that image in her mind, she can't think about it or talk about it subsequently.

By the end of the first six months, the typical infant has some understanding of object permanence, which is why she looks for a toy when it falls from her hand to a spot outside her line of immediate vision. And she will even reach for a toy that is partly hidden, perhaps half-concealed under a blanket—she knows that the complete toy is there, even though she can see only a bit of it. But let her watch you cover the toy completely with a towel and you'll see that she stops looking for it after a few seconds. It's a case of out of sight, out of mind.

A step forward in object permanence is made some time between 7 and 9 months, as the infant now starts to search for a completely concealed object. Her increased understanding and more advanced memory skills, combined with her improving representational skills, tell her that the toy is there although she can't see it. And this lays one of the foundation stones for the language explosion that is about to occur in the next few months.

Above *This baby demonstrates his increased awareness of the rings hidden under the blanket by making persistent attempts to find them.*

7–9 months

Left At 8 months this little girl is able to imitate her mother by making simple one- or two-syllable sounds or noises.

THE MAIN CHANGES TO LOOK FOR:

● **7 months** Now that her movement and understanding are more advanced, she is better able to demonstrate her comprehension of spoken language. For instance, when you say "Look at the doll," she turns in the right direction; and when she tries to reach over to get hold of the item, this proves she understands your words. She is altogether more responsive when you speak to her. This applies to your tone as well as your words, as your infant senses the different emotions in your voice.

● **8 months** She loves any form of word game and does her best to imitate the sounds that you make. You'll find that if you sing along quietly to a tune that's playing on the radio, the chances are that she will try to join in, too, and if you make a sound combination that is within her repertoire (for instance, if you say "naba" to her while she sits on your knee) she tries to make that sound herself. Language can be used for many purposes; you may find she starts to "shout" loudly when she wants to attract your attention.

● **9 months** Her sharper hearing enables her to distinguish between all the different sounds she hears. The hearing of a child of this age is usually good. She will turn her head around to the source of a noise in the room, even when it's not especially loud. Two-syllable babbles are frequent and she will begin to develop her own words for familiar people or objects. Her older brother could be "boo-pah," which might bear no resemblance to his real name but is the syllable combination she uses to refer to him.

Hearing

Language stimulation is important for your child's progress with speech. But she also needs to hear sounds clearly; otherwise she won't be able to imitate and she won't even be able to hear the sounds that she makes herself. Statistics confirm that hearing loss—whether total or partial—is the biggest cause of poor speech development in early childhood. They also confirm that approximately one child in ten has less-than-satisfactory hearing.

The typical child aged 9 months makes more sounds than she did at 6 months old. A decrease in vocalizations at this age is one possible sign of hearing loss. Another is her confusion when someone talks to her, as though she isn't sure where the voice comes from.

47

Body Language
Gestures Have Meaning

Your infant's ability to make controlled body, arm, and leg movements during this period of growth means that he can make greater use of gestures to convey his ideas. His ability to communicate his underlying feelings nonverbally—through the use of more sophisticated movements such as touching, pointing, throwing, and pushing—creates a stronger relationship with you. The more he feels you understand him, the stronger his emotional attachment to you.

These types of gestures now have three important qualities absent in his earlier movements. First, he waits for your response after he has, for example, pointed to an object or pulled at your shirt in an attempt to get your attention. He expects you to react. Second, if you don't make the required response, your infant repeats the gesture. For instance, he continues to point furiously at the object in the hope that you will understand what he wants. And third, if you don't do it for him, he tries to achieve the goal himself. After a while, for instance, he does his best to crawl across the floor to get the doll that attracted his interest originally. In other words, he says to you, "Well, if you can't be bothered to bring that to me, I suppose I'm going to have to find a way of going and getting it myself."

These three qualities typically appear in a child's body language between the ages of 7 and 9 months,

Above This little boy's total focus on his toy is shown by his fixed gaze and the way he explores every aspect of it with his hands and mouth.

and they prove his gestures are not simply random movements. Again, this demonstrates the link between the development of understanding, the growth in spoken language, and his nonverbal expressiveness.

7–9 months

GREATER VARIETY

Another significant transition in body language around this time is that your growing infant is able to express ideas, not just feelings, through nonverbal communication. Typical ideas expressed are as follows:

- **"I want to know the answer to that puzzle."** To you, there is no puzzle—the box of detergent contains soap, which you will add to the washing machine with a bundle of clothes. To your infant, however, that box of soap is one of the mysteries of life. He wants to know what it contains, what the contents taste like, and all its potential uses. So off he goes, pulling himself one way or another across the kitchen floor in a bid to reach it.

- **"I want to know how that works."** His innate desire to discover can be expressed in new ways because of his improved hand control, body movements, and vision. Nothing lies outside his sphere of interest. That important letter you happened to place beside him on the table has a magnetic influence on his curiosity. Before you know it he has crumpled it up, not because he is naughty but because he wants to investigate its properties.

- **"I think it's time for you to play with me."** One of the effects of his stronger social confidence is his willingness to initiate social interactions, instead of waiting for them to occur. So don't be surprised to find that as you stand in a supermarket line, he hands his toy to a total stranger standing beside you. This is his distinctive nonverbal way of asking the other person to join in with his game.

Left To satisfy their curiosity and build up a knowledge of the world around them, infants need to investigate and explore things with all their senses.

Not So Grumpy

An investigation closely observed a group of children aged 9 months and their parents during a wide range of play sessions, and assessed the type and frequency of nonverbal emotions expressed by the children. The results revealed that

- Each infant spent less than 5 percent of the time expressing negative feelings and almost 15 percent of the time expressing positive emotions.
- Around 70 percent of the negative emotions were mild. Extreme negative expression occurred less than 5 percent of the time.
- The average length of time an infant took to express his emotions nonverbally—whether negative or positive—was just under three seconds.

This suggests your infant is probably not as grumpy as you think!

49

Top Tips to Help Your Child

Encourage Talking

- **Imitation** When she is in a playful mood, sit her so that you are face-to-face and then chat to her to stimulate her vocalizations. Wait until she makes a sound combination such as "baba," "meh-meh," or "wohwoh." Repeat it to her, with a big smile on your face. She's delighted to realize that you are using her sounds.

- **Name everyday household objects** Your infant gradually learns the connection between the words you use and the objects you refer to when you use these words. Make a point of explaining to her that this is a hairbrush or that is a cup. Remember that she understands more than she can say.

- **Give her picture books** Your infant recognizes some familiar objects when she sees them in a picture book, although this is more difficult for her than you probably think. Point to each picture as you turn the pages, say the name of the object, and then point to the real object if it is in front of her.

- **Ask simple questions** By now there will be a number of objects and people that are part of her everyday life, such as a cup, a toy, socks, milk, her sibling, your pet dog. Ask her basic questions about these familiar objects, such as "Where is your cup?" or "Shall we play with the toy?" This extends her language.

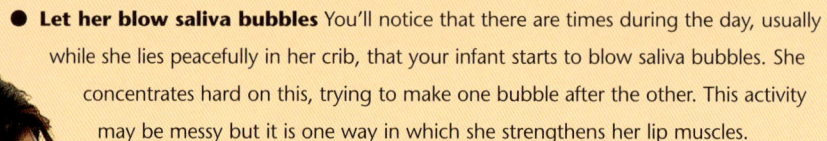

- **Let her blow saliva bubbles** You'll notice that there are times during the day, usually while she lies peacefully in her crib, that your infant starts to blow saliva bubbles. She concentrates hard on this, trying to make one bubble after the other. This activity may be messy but it is one way in which she strengthens her lip muscles.

- **Sing songs with noises** She likes to hear a poem or song that has obvious variety in it—that's why songs like "Old McDonald had a farm" is one of her favorites. She listens carefully to each different sound and, if you encourage her to join in with you, she tries to imitate them herself.

- **Watch television together** She will be less distracted and pay more attention when she feels secure and confident in your presence.

7 – 9 months

Use and Interpret Body Language

- **Play peek-a-boo games** Your infant has great fun with this type of game, even though it involves only movements. Let her see you hide your face behind your hands, and then suddenly pop your face out from one side. She might smile or she might burst into tears with fright. She would happily play this all day with you.

- **Help her search** Now that she understands object permanence, assist her when you think she is looking for an item. Suggest to her where it might be and either take her there to look for it or let her see you make the search. This encourages her to maintain her concentration and interest for longer periods.

- **Use loving gestures** Caring physical contact is an effective way of communicating loving emotions without saying a word. A gentle stroke of her cheek, a soft rub of her hair, and a quiet cuddle are very important to your infant. These gestures reassure her because she knows that they mean you love her.

- **Watch her closely** As the range of emotions expressed through body language increases with age, you may need to study your infant's facial expressions more closely than before to be sure of what she is trying to communicate to you. Be prepared to study her expressions for a while to find out what she feels.

- **Verbalize her intentions** Sometimes your 9-month-old infant will try to grab something that is beyond her reach and groan or cry with frustration. Tell her you understand what she feels by saying to her, for example, "It's annoying when you want something and can't get it."

- **Calm her anxieties** Her crying is less frequent, less unpredictable. So, when she cries at this age there is usually something significant troubling her. Do your best to calm her. Perhaps she is in tears because a stranger spoke unkindly to her or because that annoying shape won't go into the hole in her shape sorter.

- **Massage her feet** The soles of your infant's feet are very sensitive to gentle massage strokes. Most babies find this extremely relaxing and pleasurable. Neither of you need to say a word to each other, and yet your physical interactions using touch alone will bring you closer together.

Toys Unbreakable child-safe mirror with easy-to-grip edge ● soft chewy ball that is safe to mouth ● rattle that attaches to the high chair or stroller ● soft storybooks with large pictures ● wide range of music tapes and CDs ● toys with smaller pieces fitting into the main part ● wooden shape sorter ● bath toys ● large rings that stack on a pillar

Questions and Answers

Q I find that if my child gestures that he wants something, he gives up quickly if I don't understand exactly what he wants. What should I do?

A Some children are more determined to communicate than others. Personality plays a part in body language, too. It seems as though your infant isn't prepared to make an effort if you don't grasp his message the first time. Stay calm. Do your best to encourage him to use the gesture again perhaps by asking him "Is this what you want?" as you lift different objects. You may find that if you show persistence, he will respond with persistence, too, until you have fully understood what he tried to tell you.

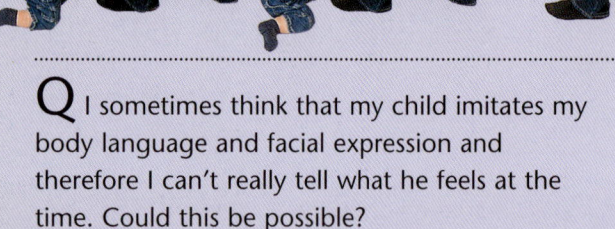

Q I sometimes think that my child imitates my body language and facial expression and therefore I can't really tell what he feels at the time. Could this be possible?

A Studies have found that imitation of a parent's emotion (as indicated by facial expression) starts between the ages of 7 and 9 months. You'll notice this even more when you and your child are in an unfamiliar situation, such as a roomful of people he doesn't know, or when you take him on a train for the first time. His natural reaction is to look at your face for reassurance. If he sees you are happy, his face instinctively reflects this feeling; if he sees that you are afraid, he looks as if he is afraid, too.

Q This may sound strange, but I'm sure my child uses sounds that are unrecognizable as part of our language. He is 8 months old. Could I just be mishearing what he says?

A Psychologists studying the babbling used by babies from many different countries have made a remarkable discovery: irrespective of their country of origin, babies tend to make the same range of babbling sounds. Of course, what happens during the first year of life is that the infant drops the sounds he doesn't hear used by those around him, and increases those that he hears regularly. So your son will soon stop using those sounds that are foreign to you and will use only those that are part of his own language system.

7–9 months

Q What is the connection between babbling and a child's first word?

A The precise relationship between these two phases of language development is unclear. For instance, although your child's controlled babbling right now involves a wide range of sounds, you'll discover that only a few of these sounds continue when he starts to say his first words. Also infants who are deaf often babble at a good rate, yet are typically unable to progress to using words and sentences without help. This suggests the relationship is tenuous. On the other hand, studies have found that babies whose babbling increases earlier than others also tend to have more developed learning skills later on, suggesting that babbling is not completely unconnected with other aspects of growth.

Q I am worried because my 7-month-old son's language is not developing as fast as his sister's did when she was that age. Or should I not compare them?

A All children are different and progress with language skills at their own rate, so comparisons between siblings are not always helpful. There is a wide range of individual difference within the boundaries of normal growth. In addition, evidence suggests that in general boys acquire language at a slower rate than girls. At this stage in your infant's development, it's extremely difficult to make long-term predictions about his future progress with the spoken word. In the meantime, therefore, stop comparing him with his sister (this only creates unnecessary anxiety) and direct your efforts toward stimulating his language skills.

Q Although she has no spoken language yet, my 9-month-old has no problem letting me know when she is about to explode with frustration. How can I help her release these feelings without having a tantrum?

A Frustration is common at this age, and because she can't yet express her inner tension with words, body language is the only way to release her annoyance. You'll already be aware of the situations that frequently lead to her frustration, such as playing with a puzzle in which the pieces have to fit exactly. Watch her in these circumstances, and try to defuse her temper before it builds up. For instance, distract her attention when you see her struggling with a toy—she can always return to it later when she is calm.

Development

7 Month Skills

MOVEMENT
- Rolls competently from back to front and vice versa.
- More consistently draws one knee toward her tummy in a crawling movement.
- May be able to move along the floor with her tummy raised.
- Takes her own weight when supported under her arms.
- Often brings feet to her mouth to suck on her toes.

HAND–EYE COORDINATION
- Explores toys in new and interesting ways by rattling, shaking, and banging them.
- Pulls at different parts of a toy.
- Has a good firm grasp and is less likely to drop a held object.
- Is more accurate when using her fingers to feed herself.
- Begins to use finger and thumb in a pincer movement.
- Uses her hands to explore her own, and others', faces.

8 Month Skills

MOVEMENT
- Has improved leg and foot strength so tries more adventurous balancing.
- Takes her own weight, gripping a chair for support.
- Able to crawl forward and backward.
- Pulls herself to standing, although she finds it hard work.

HAND–EYE COORDINATION
- Uses finger and thumb together in a pincer grip.
- Opens and closes hands voluntarily.
- Likes to drop objects when sitting in her high chair.
- Tries to pull at a string that is attached to a toy.

LANGUAGE
- Tries to imitate the sounds you make.
- Repeats the same sound over and over, such as syllables of words you use.
- Opens and closes her mouth when she watches you eat, imitating your jaw action.
- Shouts to attract your attention.

LEARNING
- Looks for a concealed object.
- Facial expression shows she recognizes a toy not seen for a couple of weeks.
- Plays with two or more toys together.
- Curious about new items.
- Discovers new properties in familiar toys; the ball she chews will roll away if pushed.
- Makes an effort to reach objects some distance away from her.
- Begins to mimic actions of others, such as waving.

9 Month Skills

MOVEMENT
- Can turn around while crawling.
- Moves her entire body comfortably around the room.
- Makes a stepping response when held under the arms.
- Shows interest in climbing up stairs.

HAND–EYE COORDINATION
- Uses a firm pincer movement to feed herself finger food such as peas and raisins.
- Hand movements are more coordinated: she may be able to build a two-brick tower.
- Brings her hands together deliberately.
- Scans her surroundings and attends to small details.
- May be able to point to an object that she wants.

LANGUAGE
- Uses two-syllable babbles consistently, such as "dada," "mama."
- Listens when you speak to her and can understand simple instructions.
- Will interrupt play to find the source of a particular sound such as a bell.
- May be able to imitate animal sounds you make to her.

LEARNING
- Loves to feel the texture of objects.
- Arranges small toys into different patterns and shapes.
- Bangs two small toys together to make sounds.
- Waves her hands in response to someone waving at her.

7 – 9 months

LANGUAGE
- More responsive when you talk to her and will respond to comments such as "Look at that."
- Likes to hear songs and to babble along with them.
- Seems to understand your different voice tones, such as happy, serious, surprised.
- Has a clear understanding of a firmly spoken "no."
- Enjoys blowing raspberries.

LEARNING
- Remembers faces of familiar adults she does not see very frequently, such as a baby-sitter.
- Continues to look for an object that goes out of her vision.
- Knows how to move toys to make them noisy.
- Understands that she can make objects move.

SOCIAL AND EMOTIONAL
- Lets you know when she's miserable or happy.
- Gets annoyed if you stop her from doing something.
- Is very aware of verbal praise and enthusiasm.
- Skilled at attracting attention when she's bored.
- Enjoys the familiarity of routines such as bathtime and bedtime.

- Is alert for longer and may manage with only one nap during the day.

SOCIAL AND EMOTIONAL
- Initiates social contact with strangers.
- Clings to you in crowded places.
- May be shy and reluctant to be picked up by strangers.
- Fascinated by mirror images and family photographs.

- Enjoys being in the presence of other babies but does not play cooperatively with them.
- May answer simple questions by facial expression, body movements, and with sounds, for example.

- Enjoys familiar games and rhymes and laughs at appropriate times.
- Makes connections between actions—for example, if she pulls the rug, the toy on it will come closer.

SOCIAL AND EMOTIONAL
- Is curious about other babies her own age and may stare or poke at another child.
- Covers her toys if another child approaches.

- Gets upset when she sees that you or other children are upset.
- Looks up at you as she plays on the floor.
- Reacts to an audience and will repeat an action that is applauded.

10–12 Months

It is during this three-month period that your child probably says his first distinct word to you. This major shift from controlled babbling to genuine words is a huge step forward in the progress of his language, signaling the start of recognizable speech development. From this moment on, his vocabulary steadily builds, providing him with a whole new range of communication possibilities. Alongside this transition are changes in body language, which arise from improvements in your child's movement skills and understanding. He is a more active, dynamic individual now, and is more able to express his feelings and thoughts in a nonverbal way.

Language Development
From Babbling to Words

A number of changes usually occur in a child's babbling as she steadily moves toward her first birthday. First, the syllable combinations she uses become noticeably more complex, now involving at least three different consonant-vowel blends. Second, the overall sound of this form of babbling conforms to the sound patterns of spoken language—it contains only consonant-vowel combinations that are used in speech. And third, the strings of babbling start to share other characteristics of spoken language, such as intonation and length of utterance.

It's as though your child talks, except that she does not use words. If you stand a few yards away from her when she babbles like this—so that you are close enough to see her, but far enough away that you can't hear her sounds clearly—the combined effect of these three features could make you think she is actually talking in sentences to you. It's only when you approach that you realize she is babbling.

The chances are that she says her first word at around 12 months old, when her understanding, maturation of her vocal cords, and general development merge together, enabling her to use genuine speech. Your child's first word need not match any existing word exactly, nor need it refer to one particular person or one particular object. What gives this sound combination the status of "first word" is that it has two clear characteristics: first, it means something specific, and second, it has a distinctive form and shape that you recognize each time you hear it.

A child's first word is often a "holophrase," which is a unit of sound that is actually a substitute for an entire sentence. For instance, "dada" might refer to her father, or it might mean, "I hear dad's car outside."

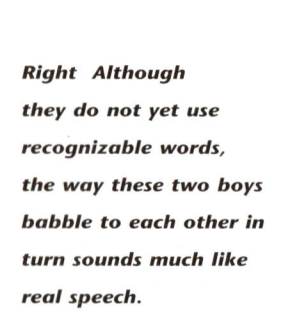

Right Although they do not yet use recognizable words, the way these two boys babble to each other in turn sounds much like real speech.

10 – 12 months

THE MAIN CHANGES TO LOOK FOR:

Above At 10 months this little boy's attention is totally focused on the balloon. A child of this age should never be left alone to play with anything that could cause choking.

● **10 months** She loves chatting to you in her own way, using various consonant-vowel babbling sounds that are combined into longer strings that may be repeated. You'll also notice that she spends more time looking at you when she talks—her awareness of the social dimensions of communication increases. Your child's attention improves, and so she now watches more closely when you point out various people and objects to her. Sometimes she gazes at an object long after you have referred to it, as though trying to absorb more information about it.

● **11 months** Language fascinates her in any form, whether it be discussion, poems, nursery rhymes, or songs. Your child can follow basic instructions—her physical response lets you know that she fully understands what you want, for instance, when you leave her for a moment to go out of the room, wave to her in an exaggerated way, and say to her, "Wave bye-bye." Although her hand–eye coordination has a long way to go, at this stage she'll probably move her hand to wave to you just as you requested. She enjoys carrying out your instructions.

Right At 11 months some children will begin to use real words in the right context. This little girl is waving and saying bye-bye.

● **12 months** A minority of children have already said their first word earlier than the twelfth month of life, but the majority achieve it now. This is a very special occasion that delights you. Your enthusiastic response when she reaches this stage encourages her to develop her language skills even further. First words rarely match the intended word exactly. Do your best to decide what the word refers to without making her repeat it or she may become reluctant to speak that word to you next time.

Word Patterns

Don't be surprised when your child's first word is incomplete. The most common "error" for a child this age is when she uses the proper starting letter of the word but then simply adds a vowel sound so that the word seems to fade away. Another common error is to leave out the opening letters—perhaps because they are too complicated for her to pronounce—and then to sound just the remaining part of the word. But these aren't really errors and therefore you shouldn't try to correct them. Look on them as inevitable steps in the process of language learning. She speaks like this because this is the best she can do. Her speech will naturally improve over the next few weeks and months.

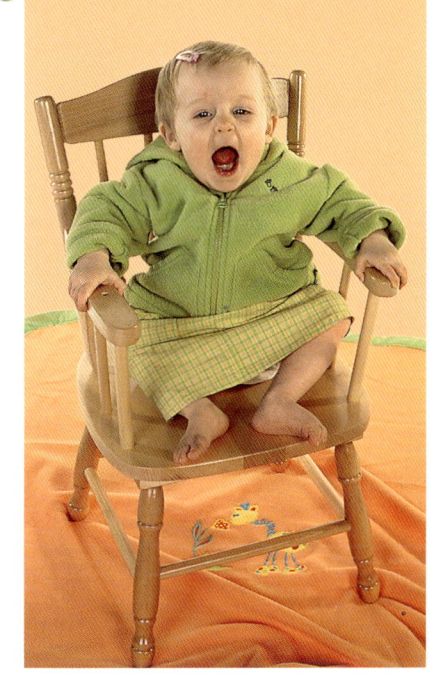

59

Body Language
Creative Body Language

In these few months before proper speech becomes a communication option for your child, he uses body language more deliberately and creatively than ever before. It's almost as if his frustration at realizing he can nearly speak (but not quite) boosts his need to use nonverbal communication intentionally. Once the spoken word takes over, his nonverbal communication can become less conscious, although it remains extremely important.

Left Once your child is walking confidently he will become increasingly determined to achieve his objectives independently.

Because there is so much that he wants to say to you because his grasp of the world around him is more sophisticated, you'll find that his body language is more dynamic, interesting, and varied. For instance, your child may try to make you laugh by deliberately hiding his cuddly toy under the blanket; he laughs loudly when he sees your sense of humor has been triggered by his actions. Or he might grab hold of your hand and pull you over to something that he wants you to look at. You'll be surprised at the creative ways he finds to say things to you nonverbally. He may even hide a book he dislikes.

This increased use of body language to express feelings and ideas is matched by your child's increased understanding of your own body language. He's more able to read your facial expressions, your mood, and temperament, and he responds accordingly. That's why you may find that when you are tired, lethargic, and feeling down in the dumps, your child is like this, too. He tries hard to read your body language and copy it.

Below By now children have a sufficient level of concentration to persevere with a challenging toy, although frustration can set in if it proves too difficult.

60

10 – 12 months

Above and right This little boy is clearly frustrated because his sister has the toy he wants, and his whole demeanor indicates his intention to snatch it back!

GREATER VARIETY

The first year has been a period of enormous emotional and psychological advances for your child. His basic needs—to be fed, to be cared for, to be loved—remain, but new emotional drives begin to dominate. As always in this prelanguage stage of development, these drives are expressed nonverbally. Expect to see the following:

● **Independence** He wants to do things by himself. When he moves away from you and attempts a difficult challenge (such as opening a drawer), these body movements, coupled with his moans and groans as he struggles to pull open the drawer, tell you what he's trying to achieve. The fact that he pushes you away when you try to help is not naughtiness; it is simply his way of insisting "I can do it on my own."

● **Frustration** You probably think temper drives your child to throw his toy against the floor. Although there may be an element of anger in that nonverbal action, the chances are that the real underlying force is frustration. Your child has not yet learned the personal skills required to cope with inability to achieve—the tension builds inside him until he releases it through arm, leg, and hand gestures.

● **Confidence** Most of the time your 1-year-old is confident, effusively moving about the house. Yet his body language occasionally reveals how fragile his confidence really is. Like the time he literally toddled behind you and tried to bury his face in the back of your legs when you answered the door to the mail carrier—he removes himself from a socially uncomfortable situation.

Gaze

Your child's gaze is an important part of his body language. His eye movements are controlled by six eye muscles that govern sweeping movements, fixations, corrections for head turning, and synchrony between the two eyes. This system is sophisticated by the end of the first year. One study found that 11-month-old infants will even follow an adult's line of vision to discover what that person is staring at. Gaze can be an effective way for your child to express aggression and threat—for instance, when he scowls at you with a penetrating stare. But it can also be welcoming, such as when he looks lovingly straight into your eyes. Psychologists claim positive mutual gazing helps the formation of an emotional connection between parent and child.

61

Top Tips to Help Your Child

Encourage Talking

- **Provide examples** Bear in mind that your child learns from your speech, even though she cannot yet say the same words herself or use the same complexity of grammar. So when she gestures toward the refrigerator indicating she wants a drink, put her request into words—for instance, "I think you'd like a drink of juice."

- **Don't confront** In your desire to hear her say her first word, you may inadvertently slip into the situation where you refuse to give her what she wants unless she says a word that sounds like the desired object. Resist this temptation, because it only creates a confrontation between you and your child. You can't force her.

- **Musical instruments** As you have already discovered, your growing child likes listening to music and even tries to sing along with some of the tunes. This enthusiasm becomes enhanced when she has the opportunity to make "music" with toy musical instruments even though her productions may sound dreadful to you.

- **Pay attention** She needs to know you listen to her, despite the fact that she still babbles and may not yet have reached her first single word. Look interested when she vocalizes to you, talk back in response to what you think she tells you, and try to match your expression to hers. Your attention stimulates her desire to speak.

- **Read her a story at night** Watching you read, and listening to the words as you speak them, further increases her interest in spoken language. She associates stories with pleasant feelings, particularly when she hears you read one as she falls asleep. Make sure, though, that you read bedtime stories that are relaxing.

- **Chat to her** Much of her language learning is incidental, in that it occurs naturally through hearing everyday language spoken around her. That's why it makes sense to talk to your child when in her company. Tell her what you are doing at the time, and talk about things she sees. Let her listen to your conversations.

- **Sing songs and recite rhymes** Aside from being pleasant to listen to, songs and poems follow a rhyming sequence. Your child begins to notice that every so often (at the end of a line) the words sound the same, and this sharpens her sound discrimination skills. You'll notice that she tries to move in time to the beat.

10 – 12 months

Use and Interpret Body Language

- **Encourage concentration** She uses her gaze more systematically than before. You can help her gain more control over her eye movements through a range of activities. For example, ask her to look at a picture book, or give her instructions involving visual searches such as "Where is the dog?" and wait for her reaction.

- **Develop her patience** Nonverbal (and eventually verbal) communication requires your child to be patient as the listener interprets her message. But patience is one quality that is usually elusive in a child this age, so calm her irritation when you don't respond immediately. Tell her, "I would like you to show me this again."

- **Vary the audience** She needs to interact with others, too. That's why she benefits from communicating nonverbally with visitors, such as her aunt and uncle or her grandparents. Ask your child to "Show grandpa your new toy" or "Smile at your uncle." She learns to make her responses more obvious to someone who doesn't know her.

- **Respond to her cuddles** Not only is she willing to receive cuddles, but she now likes to dispense them herself. This is her way of expressing affection. You might even find that she cuddles inanimate objects, such as the soft chair in which she sits to watch television or her favorite toy. When she cuddles you unexpectedly, cuddle her in return.

- **Anticipate her needs** Having lived with her for a year, you can now anticipate her emotional needs as expressed by her body language. So if you see her trying to achieve something independently, stand beside her but don't interfere. If you realize that she is becoming agitated, relax her before her frustration erupts.

- **Make "funny faces"** Humor is a significant part of your child's emotional life. She likes to laugh and to make others laugh. When you are close together and have established eye contact, make a silly face, one that causes her to howl with laughter. Then ask her to make a silly face. Laugh at her action, even if it is not amusing.

- **Use varied social gestures** Remember that your child learns new gestures and body language from you. Help her broaden her repertoire by using gestures that signal your understanding. For instance, look at her when she babbles or talks, nod your head slowly when you know what she means, and furrow your brow when she's upset.

Toys Wind-up music toy ● storybooks with simple pictures ● set of small plastic toy animals ● toy wooden telephone with receiver ● lots of cuddly soft toys ● wooden inset boards with one or two pieces ● doll with clothes that are easily removed ● large plastic construction blocks ● pull-along toy on wheels ● plastic alphabet play mat with brightly colored patterns ● unbreakable child's mirror with easy-to-grip edge

Questions and Answers

Q My child has said his first word, but I'm upset because it wasn't "mama" or "daddy." Am I being silly reacting in this way?

A What matters is that your child has said his first word, not the actual word itself. There are two reasons why "mama" and "dadda" are often first words: parents naturally encourage their child to say these words and repeat them many times to him, and these words are easy for a child to pronounce. You are probably upset because you think that this means he doesn't love you as much as you thought, but put this idea out of your mind completely. Whether or not he uses "mama" or "dadda" as his first word has no bearing whatsoever on the strength of his emotional bond with you.

Q My 11-month-old child loves to suck a pacifier during the day. Could this habit have a bad effect on his language development?

A Sucking the pacifier has emotional benefits for your child—he feels happier and more relaxed when he has a comforter in his mouth, and this can make the day easier for both of you. On the other hand, it does restrict the range of movements that he can make with his lips, tongue, and throat muscles, and it also means that he doesn't babble while sucking the pacifier. To this extent, the use of a pacifier cannot make a positive contribution to his speech progress. The best strategy is to limit the amount of time for which he sucks it during the day.

Q How can I be expected to interpret my 10-month-old infant's body language when he is so passive? He sits there with very little expression on his face.

A Some children are more expressive than others, whether using spoken language or body language. The desire to communicate depends partly on personality. It appears that your child's natural tendency is to be less communicative than you would normally expect. He may become more open once he acquires spoken language, but in the meantime you have to work with the communication skills he has, whatever they may be. The expression on his face may be mainly neutral, but try to interpret it anyway. And maybe he rarely uses gestures, but make the most of them when he does.

10 – 12 months

Q What can I do to curb my child's aggression to others? When I take him to parent-and-toddler group, he grabs toys without saying a word.

A The problem he faces is that he wants to play with a toy that he doesn't possess at the time, but he doesn't have the language skills (or the social skills) to ask politely for it. The only avenue open to him is to express his wishes nonverbally, and hence he snatches the object without any concern for his peers. Help him become more sensitive by discouraging this habit. Remove the toy from his hands and let him see you return it to its original owner. Explain to him why you are doing this and try to calm him.

Q Is it possible that my 10-month-old infant recognizes the names of other people in the family, and even the names of other people he sees only occasionally?

A Yes, it is entirely possible. Your child's recognition of people's names depends on a number of factors, the most important of which is "salience"—in other words, the extent to which the person is psychologically important to him. That's why he may remember the name of someone he sees only periodically if this person is very special to him or if they usually share a special activity together. Another important factor regarding recognition of names is the name itself. One that is short and simple with only a few letters is easier for your infant to recognize than a lengthy name.

Q No matter how often I leave my child with a baby-sitter, she absolutely howls when I leave and stares pathetically at me. What can I do to reduce her tears?

A You will find that her heartbreaking tears gradually decrease in intensity as her experience of separating from you builds up, if you manage these moments firmly yet lovingly. However, if you make a terrible fuss over your child at the point at which she starts crying, and then prolong the moment of separation with lots of cuddles and words of reassurance, her tearful episodes will continue. That's why it is best to give her a quick, comforting hug when the baby-sitter arrives—whether she cries or not—then put on your coat and leave without lingering unnecessarily.

Development

10 Month Skills

MOVEMENT
- Likes looking at the world from an upright position.
- Good at crawling and able to propel herself along the floor.
- Climbs up the first step of the stairs and slides down from it.
- Stands on her own two feet, gripping something for support.

HAND–EYE COORDINATION
- Likes playing with toys that move across the floor.
- Likes to explore insides of boxes, cupboards, and drawers.
- Grips two small blocks in one hand.
- Hand preference may begin to show.
- Enjoys rhymes involving hand coordination, such as "Pat-a-cake."

LANGUAGE
- Combines different syllables in one utterance, for example "ah-leh," "muh-gah."

11 Month Skills

MOVEMENT
- Moves swiftly around the room, supporting herself with the furniture.
- Slowly and gently lowers herself to the ground, landing with only a small bump.
- May bottom-shuffle around the room.
- May lean toward an object on the floor while standing against a support.

HAND–EYE COORDINATION
- Is fascinated by containers and shakes them in the air.
- Tries to pull lids off boxes to find whatever is inside them.
- Shows good coordination of thumb and index finger.
- Turns pages of a book as you sit and read with her.
- Enjoys putting one thing into another.
- May be able to build a small tower of stacking cups or blocks.

LANGUAGE
- Listens to you very carefully when you talk to her.
- Follows simple instructions, for instance to give things and take them back.
- Occasionally utters single words but much of her language appears meaningless.
- Enjoys playing with musical toys and experimenting with her own sounds to accompany them.
- Will point to an object in a picture book when you say its name.

LEARNING
- With better concentration she can focus on an activity for at least a minute.

12 Month Skills

MOVEMENT
- Early signs of independent walking.
- More confident climbing up the stairs.
- Has better body control when lowering herself from standing.
- Crawls effectively on hands and knees.
- May walk if you hold her hands or when she is pushing a wheeled toy.

HAND–EYE COORDINATION
- May use a spoon for stirring rather than banging.
- Builds with small wooden blocks.
- Enjoys water games and can pour from containers held in left or right hand.
- Can slot simple shapes correctly into a shape sorter.
- May be able to make a mark on paper with a crayon.
- Hand preference is more obvious.

LANGUAGE
- Has said her first word: "dadda" is commonly first, or "bye-bye."
- May be able to use three or four words to name familiar objects, such as "dog."

10 – 12 months

- Stops what she is doing and listens when you say her name.
- Says one or two words consistently, not always clearly.
- Chatters in the rhythm of speech but without meaning.
- Moves her body along to the rhythm of music.

LEARNING
- Tries to imitate your actions.
- Is interested in things that go together, such as cup and saucer and parts of puzzles.
- Listens to and follows basic instructions such as "Give me the cup."
- Likes trying to push shapes into a shape sorter.
- Spends up to a fifth of her waking time staring and observing.

SOCIAL AND EMOTIONAL
- Gives cuddles as well as receiving them.
- Loves playing interactive games, like peek-a-boo.
- Is happy to spend time amusing herself.
- May be anxious when visiting unfamiliar places.
- Snuggles up to you when you read her a story.
- Has no understanding of the effect of her actions on other children.

- Can place blocks in a plastic cup.
- Imitates more of your actions as you move around the house.
- Tries something, then reflects on her actions for a few moments.
- May attempt the next action in a familiar routine that you have begun.

SOCIAL AND EMOTIONAL
- Is frustrated when her wishes are blocked and loses her temper quite easily.
- Swings from positive to negative moods very quickly.
- Stares at other children but does not interact with them.
- Likes to do things that gain your approval.
- Feels very secure with you but anxious with unfamiliar people.

- Follows basic instructions consistently.
- Has good hearing but loses interest in repetitive sounds.
- Knows the names of other members of the family.

LEARNING
- Understands basic directions involving one familiar action, such as "Wave bye-bye."
- Copies you when you bang two wooden blocks together.
- Is curious about objects that rattle.
- Makes a good effort to put the pieces of an inset board in place.
- May hesitate when given a new puzzle but will then apply existing knowledge.
- Needs less sleep and may be awake for about 11 hours every day.

SOCIAL AND EMOTIONAL
- Plays any games that involve social interaction between you and her.
- Is very affectionate toward you and others in her family.
- May show her temper when she doesn't want to cooperate with others.
- Has a preference for playing with a child of her own gender when in mixed groups.
- Will play next to another baby her age, but will play actively with an older child.
- Has tremendous belief in her own abilities and is increasingly frustrated when she finds she can't achieve her chosen goals.

67

13–15 Months

Spoken language improves steadily now, and if your child has not said his first word by the time he reaches his first birthday, the chances are that he will do so by the time he is 15 months old. The most significant step forward during this period is the gradual buildup of single words that he uses. Understanding improves, too—although his speech is limited, he understands a lot more of what you say to him. Now that he communicates more directly through verbal language, his body language becomes more subtle and can often be more revealing than before about his thoughts and feelings.

Language Development
Early Vocabulary

The rate at which your child acquires new words in the three months after her first word may be slower than you would expect. She might add only six or seven new words to her spoken vocabulary during this period, or possibly a few more. Although this slow rate of speech development—and the range of words she uses—is in marked contrast to the vast array of sounds that constantly appeared in the previous stage of babbling, the reduction in pace is a universal phenomenon found in virtually all children.

One major psychological investigation examined the types of words used by children in their early vocabularies and classified these into six categories, along with their frequency of use:

● **General nominals** These refer to groups or classes of objects, animals, or people (such as "milk," "car")—52 percent.

● **Specific nominals** These refer to a specific object, animal, or person (such as "mama," "dadda")—14 percent.

● **Action words** These refer to actions that the child makes (such as "up") or that accompany actions she makes (such as "bye")—13 percent.

● **Modifiers** These are early adjectives, words that describe the qualities of an object, animal, or person (such as "big," "mine")—9 percent.

● **Personal social words** These refer to the child's feelings or to her relationships (such as "want," "please")—8 percent.

● **Function words** These are words that have only a grammatical purpose and don't mean anything individually (such as "what," "to")—4 percent.

Although most of your child's words between 13 and 15 months are specific and general nominals, some of the other types of words appear, too. She also prefers to use words connected with actions that she can manage, such as eating and playing. And she is unlikely to refer to items that are either immobile or that she cannot manipulate herself.

Early vocabulary, therefore, is strongly connected to her own needs.

Below Once your child has a few basic words for familiar objects, he will enjoy pointing them out to you when he comes across them.

13 – 15 months

THE MAIN CHANGES TO LOOK FOR:

● **13 months** She likes action rhymes whose endings she anticipates with great delight, such as "This little piggy"—she giggles before you even reach the part where you tickle her. These activities provide such enjoyment because they enable her to participate using language and other skills she already has. And the great aspect of this type of play is that your toddler begins to associate language with fun, increasing her determination to speak herself.

● **14 months** When your child hears songs, nursery rhymes, and poems, she likes to take an active role. Of course there are times when she still likes to listen to spoken language—such as at story time or when she watches a video—because she finds these interesting and relaxing. But she is more active with language now, so when you sing a familiar song she wants to join in to some extent. Leave out the last word of each line, and pause when you come to that word—she will probably make an attempt to say it herself.

● **15 months** Most children can say around seven or eight single words at this age. Now that she has been speaking for several weeks, her pronunciation is clearer and you know what she means when she uses them. Don't expect her to combine words into a phrase, however, because that stage does not arrive until later. Your child's general understanding is more advanced than her spoken language, and as a result her frustration may actually increase during this period. She wants to say more than her vocabulary allows.

Above Action songs and rhymes will delight your child, and as she gets to know them well she will start to join in with the words.

Right At this age children will often try to say things that their limited vocabulary cannot stretch to, although parents can often translate correctly!

Word Bias

Researchers have shown that a child's understanding of words is influenced by a number of automatic "biases":

• Whole object bias: A child's tendency when hearing a new word to attach that word to the whole object, not only to part of it: she assumes that "table" refers to the entire object and not just, say, to the legs.

• Taxonomic bias: A child's tendency to assume that the word describes a class of objects, not just that particular object: she assumes that "car" refers to all items with that appearance.

• Mutual exclusivity bias: A child's tendency to use only one word to describe an object: if she hears someone use a different word for a table, she assumes that person is referring to something else.

71

Body Language
Expressing Emotion Nonverbally

Children this age continue to use nonverbal means—such as facial expression, muscle tension, posture, breathing, and noises—to express emotion just as much as they did before, despite the onset of spoken language. The position changes around the fifteenth month, when emotional words begin to enter a child's vocabulary, resulting in body language becoming more subtle.

Right *When your child is really upset he will revert to actions rather than words to communicate his feelings and, as with a baby, you need to interpret and respond appropriately.*

Below *At this age children cannot always identify, let alone express, the source of their discomfort, and that is why your understanding of their behavior is still so vital.*

When a child has only a few basic words, he tends to use these words when his body language reveals that he has a positive feeling. Nonverbal signs of negative feelings, on the other hand, are rarely accompanied by words. It's almost as though an infant's negative emotions are so intense that he instinctively releases them through body language instead of trying to find appropriate words.

Another critical factor encouraging the survival of your child's body language during this three-month period is your continued response to his nonverbal communication, even though you are desperate for him to speak to you. Studies have found that parents intuitively react to their child's positive body language by mirroring that feeling—so a parent typically smiles, relaxes, and breathes easily when their child is clearly happy. And when a child displays negative body language, parents tend to carry out a physical action, such as removing the source of the child's discomfort.

Both these types of responses—either reflecting your child's own body language or doing something to relieve his emotional discomfort—reinforce his developing use of nonverbal communication and ensure that he continues to use body language to express emotions no matter how sophisticated his spoken language becomes.

13 – 15 months

CURIOSITY

Your toddler's desire to learn accelerates, partly because his understanding of the world is more advanced and partly because he can move around without your help. But his intentions are not always obvious and you can easily mistake his natural explorations for deliberate misbehavior. Here are ways in which your toddler's body language tells you "I'm curious, not naughty":

Below Even though words are now part of your child's life, much of his exploring is still through touch; just looking does not give him all the information he needs.

● Frowning facial expression

Sometimes a frown can signify anger, but with a toddler between the ages of 13 and 15 months it probably means that he is puzzled about what he sees. His eye muscles tighten up, his brow suddenly contains wrinkle lines, and his lips pucker slightly.

● Sloping body posture

When a person's body leans forward during a conversation it often indicates aggression. In this instance, though, it is a sign of your child's curiosity. He realizes that the closer his face is to the object or person that attracts his attention, the more he sees of it.

● Poking and touching

Learning at this age involves physical manipulation. Your child needs to feel an object, hold it in his hands, and turn it around to satisfy his curiosity. His handling of items may agitate you—especially if they are fragile—but this is the way he discovers new things.

● Pulling your hand

He may be afraid to approach something or someone unfamiliar, even though he wants to know more, and so he decides to take you along—your presence boosts his confidence. He grabs your hand and pulls you along with him.

Toddler Stares

Older children and adults learn two important aspects of body language. First, staring is regarded as impolite and unwelcome. Second, personal space—that is, the actual distance separating two people in a conversation—is normally about 18 inches. When either of these nonverbal conventions is breached, the other person feels uncomfortable. And yet your toddler's instinct is to ignore these conventions when he wants to learn more about someone. When he sees someone in a wheelchair, for instance, his instinct is to stand as close to this person as he possibly can and stare unflinchingly into their face, leaving you totally embarrassed and apologetic about his behavior. Explain to him why he should act more sensitively.

73

Top Tips to Help Your Child

Encourage Talking

- **Initiate pretend play** She may be ready to use her imagination in some form of pretend play, especially when you start the game off. Hold one of her dolls in your arms as though it is a baby, talk to it, and pretend to feed it from a plastic cup. Give your toddler a cup and a doll—she copies you.

- **Name body parts** Hold her hand in yours and say, "This is your hand." Do the same with her other hand, too. Make sure she looks at her hands as you speak. Then do this with her feet. You'll find she learns the names of different body parts, as long as you teach one at a time.

- **Encourage her listening skills** When you and your child hear a noise from outside, stop what you are doing and pause—tell her to listen. Then ask her what the noise could be. She might say an appropriate word such as "car"; whether she does or not, take her outside to find the source of the noise.

- **Talk about the stories you read** When you read her a story during the day, talk about it with her once you have finished it. Remind her of the key features, such as the name of the central character. Select a couple of action points from the story that she particularly enjoyed and go over them again.

- **Respond to gestures with words** By now you know what she means when she points to the pantry—she wants something to eat. But don't simply respond silently. Say to her, for instance, "I can see you would like something to eat." This builds an association between gestures and words.

- **Use words that describe differences** Although your toddler has some understanding of the difference between, say, "big" and "small," she has not yet grasped the words that are used to describe these qualities—and she will not master that skill until she is older. Yet you can start the process of learning comparison words by pointing out obvious differences in, say, size or height.

- **Respond positively to each new word** A new word slips into her vocabulary without any warning. She suddenly starts to use it, as if it has been part of her speech all the time. Don't hide your excitement when you hear the addition to her word range, because your delight encourages her.

13 – 15 months

Use and Interpret Body Language

- **Be patient** Now that she is more active and is an independent walker, you may find your patience is taxed as you seem to spend a lot of time trying to keep track of her movements. Resist the temptation to get annoyed with her journeys. This is simply her way of expressing her desire to investigate her surroundings.

- **Sort out arguments** Toddlers are notoriously self-interested, thinking only of themselves and showing no sensitivity to others, which is why bickering is so common between children of this age. When your child gets into a tussle with one of her peers, quickly remove her from the spot and try to calm her.

- **Avoid challenges that are too hard** Your ambitious toddler wants to make new achievements, but challenges that are too difficult may sap her motivation. You can tell by her body language whether she has become de-motivated—her shoulders sag, she looks down, and her limbs flop. That means it's time to find something easier for her to do.

- **Aid moves to independence** When you see her trying to complete an activity on her own, give her lots of encouragement. Do not take over, however. Your toddler is motivated to manage by herself and she doesn't want you to do everything for her. The best way to help is by showing her different strategies for reaching her target.

- **Provide dress-up clothes** With the onset of imagination, she likes putting on your old clothes. Fill an old cardboard box with clothes that your child can wear, such as shoes, sweaters, and hats. She doesn't say anything when holding them, but the expression on her face tells you that her imagination has been fired by them.

- **Watch for fear reactions** The onset of fears is very common at this age. Surveys have found that toddlers usually have at least one fear, such as anxiety about small animals or insects. Remain calm when you see your child afraid, give her lots of reassurance, and then just continue with what you and she were doing before.

- **Provide social opportunities** One of the ways she learns new methods of expressing herself through body language is by watching other children. If possible, take her to a parent-and-toddler group. Aside from the social benefits, attendance at this type of group will enable her to observe the way that others use nonverbal communication.

Toys jack-in-the-box ● toy musical instruments ● plastic or wooden train with lots of rail cars ● cassette tape of animal noises ● various soft toys and small dolls ● plastic book with pictures ● pull-along toy on wheels ● thick colored crayons and white paper ● plastic or wooden construction blocks ● boxes of colored play dough ● large sand and water tray

Questions and Answers

Q Why is it that my child shouts so much? It's as if using a very loud voice is his natural way of speaking, and I find myself speaking loudly back to him.

A He probably just enjoys hearing himself say the words—remember that his developing speech is as exciting for your child as it is for you. You'll find that the volume of his words spontaneously decreases over the next year. In the meantime, however, you can try to hasten the process along by responding in a quiet voice. Don't talk loudly when he does. Instead, use a register that is slightly lower than the normal volume you use. Your toddler will moderate his volume to come into line with the volume of your speech.

Q When my toddler gets angry or concentrates, he makes bizarre facial expressions. I'm worried that others will laugh at him if he continues to make such odd-looking facial contortions when he is older.

A At this age, your child's emotions are expressed without reservation. So when there is any shift in mood, either positive or negative, his instinct is to communicate this immediately through facial expression. In addition, he lacks social awareness and is unconcerned about the impressions he makes. These are the reasons his facial expressions are so extreme. During the preschool years, however, the situation changes. First, he gains more control over his strong emotions, and second, he becomes aware that others look at him, resulting in more appropriate, less unusual, facial expressions.

Q My 4-year-old is very caring toward his sister, who is only 14 months, and he continues to speak for her even though she has started to talk. Will this slow down her speech development?

A Your toddler needs every encouragement to develop her own spoken language. Although it's great that your older child is so caring toward her, his readiness to explain on her behalf what she wants may actually have a negative effect in the long term—she may not feel the need to speak herself. Discuss this with your 4-year-old. Explain gently that you are delighted he is such a caring brother, but add that he can help his sister more by allowing her to talk. Then cuddle him for being a wonderful big brother.

13 – 15 months

Q Our 13-month-old toddler prefers to play with his father when he comes home rather than with me. When I try to play with him at that time, he pushes me away without saying a word and goes to my partner. Does this mean he doesn't like me?

A There are other more probable interpretations of this action, so don't assume that your toddler dislikes you. What is much more likely is that because your toddler spends all day with you, he is very excited when his father arrives home and he wants to play exclusively with him at that moment. That's a typical reaction of a toddler toward a parent who is away from the house during the day. So your 13-month-old's body language is saying that he loves his father, not that he dislikes you.

Q My toddler is 14 months old. He has recently started to cry whenever I switch off his bedroom light. Does this mean he is afraid of the dark?

A This could be an accurate interpretation of his body language. Put your idea to the test. Leave his bedroom light on at night. If you find his tears stop, then he probably is afraid of the dark. If he continues to cry even though the light is on, then his body language indicates that he has some other concern. For instance, he may not like being separated from you at night and cries from this temporary unhappiness, or maybe he finds his bedroom boring because he doesn't have toys close at hand to play with. Check out all the possibilities.

Q My child is 15 months old and yet doesn't utter a word. All her friends said their first word months ago. What should I do?

A There is huge variation in the timing of a child's first word, and there are plenty of children who pass the 15-month mark without that elusive language milestone having appeared. One way to reassure yourself is by considering other positive signs of satisfactory language development. For instance, if she babbles at you in a controlled way throughout the day, if her hearing is good and she turns around when a noise is made close by, if she tries to join in with songs and rhymes— then her speech progress is fine and she'll probably say her first word any time now.

Development

13 Month Skills

MOVEMENT
- Spends a lot of time trying to climb up stairs but finds coming down is harder.
- Steadier on her feet, though still topples easily.
- Might rely on a chair or wheeled toy for support when walking.
- Is determined to walk on her own, despite frequent falls.

HAND–EYE COORDINATION
- Uses her hand to indicate to you that she wants a particular object.
- Enjoys making marks on paper with crayons and pencils.
- Hits pegs into a peg board with a hammer.
- Plays with a toy telephone, putting the receiver on and off it.

LANGUAGE
- Recognizes her own name but probably cannot say it.
- Says five or six words in the appropriate context.
- Shouts out at you when she doesn't like what you are doing.
- Makes tuneful sounds when hearing familiar music.

LEARNING
- Will try to use a spoon to feed herself.
- Has fun pointing to pictures of familiar objects in books.
- Will concentrate for longer periods on puzzle toys.
- Interested in videotapes and television programs.
- Begins to show imagination in play.

14 Month Skills

MOVEMENT
- Totters about the house, tripping over objects on the floor.
- Is able to stop and change direction when walking.
- Insists on walking unaided when outside with you.
- Climbs stairs on all fours or by shifting her bottom one step at a time.
- May still crawl occasionally although she can walk.

HAND–EYE COORDINATION
- Knows how to use crayons appropriately instead of mouthing them.
- Can build a tower of three bricks.
- Is more adept at fitting difficult pieces into a shape sorter.
- Puts her hands and arms up when you bring her pullover toward her.
- May be able to throw a medium-sized, lightweight ball.

LANGUAGE
- Tries to sing along with you.
- Begins to learn names of body parts.
- Listens avidly to other children when they talk to each other.
- Enjoys making sounds with musical instruments.
- Her babbling has all the rhythm of language.
- Is fascinated by the language use of other children the same age.

LEARNING
- Can complete a simple but lengthy task with encouragement.

15 Month Skills

MOVEMENT
- Moves confidently through the house.
- Has better balance as she walks, keeping her arms closer to her sides.
- Can stop when walking and bend to pick up an object from the floor.
- Attempts to stand still and kick a ball if encouraged to do so—but will probably miss or fall backward.
- Masters the challenge of climbing in and out of her high chair.
- May be able to kneel on a chair while at a table.

HAND–EYE COORDINATION
- Is able to hold two items in each hand at the same time.
- Has a firm hand grip and rarely drops objects accidentally.
- Likes playing with moving objects, watching them as they roll.
- Enjoys fitting pieces into an inset board or puzzle.

13 – 15 months

SOCIAL AND EMOTIONAL
- Innate desire to become independent begins to show. For example, she tries to help when being dressed.
- Is less inclined to go for an afternoon nap.
- Will give you a big cuddle when she is happy.
- Holds a cup and drinks from it, with some help.
- May pass toys to another child.
- Plays alongside rather than with a child of her age.

- Can look away from what she is doing, then go back to it.
- Is eager to explore the whole house but is oblivious to danger.
- Has a serious facial expression while you read her a story.
- Is developing the use of imagination in play, for example with pretend tea parties.

SOCIAL AND EMOTIONAL
- Is more socially confident yet is sometimes terrified of strangers.
- Has increased sense of self and awareness that she is an individual with her own likes and dislikes.
- Recognizes that her name is different from other people's.
- May develop a minor fear, for example, of animals.
- Loves to be independent and to cope without your help.
- May have a temporary phase of attachment to one parent in particular.

LANGUAGE
- Can say seven or eight single words.
- Understands many more words than she can say.
- Has great fun when you recite familiar rhymes and songs to her.
- Can follow a broader range of basic instructions, such as "Let go of the toy."

LEARNING
- Concentrates well until she completes an activity.
- Enjoys pretend play, alone or with you.
- Will try to put away her toys if instructed to do so.
- Enjoys sand and water play.

SOCIAL AND EMOTIONAL
- Is very determined to get her own way.
- Has a tantrum when her frustrations become too much.
- Wants to feed herself, though she can't manage entirely on her own.
- Is eager to explore everything whether it is safe or not.
- Begins to show signs of jealousy when you give attention to others.
- Loves the social nature of a family meal.
- Can begin to learn social skills, such as greeting another person by saying "hello."

79

16–18 Months

Your child's use of single words steadily increases during this period, and he may reach the point of rapid vocabulary growth in which the extent of his spoken vocabulary increases from seven or eight words to more than twenty words. This rather unexpected leap in his use of language happens spontaneously and often (though not always) coincides with his ability to use two words together to form a meaningful phrase. Corresponding changes occur in his body language, too; nonverbal communication becomes less voluntary because spoken communication dominates, but when your toddler deliberately uses body language it may be exaggerated.

Language Development
First Words

Be patient with your child during this period. The average time between her first word and establishing a vocabulary of ten words is around three months. This means you'll hear an awful lot of repetition! Try not to let her see that you find her limited vocabulary slightly taxing. Remember that the frequent use of the same words over and over again provides a solid foundation for subsequent vocabulary growth.

One way of analyzing a child's use of language at this stage is to look at her "vocabulary strategy"—in other words, look at the main focus of her words. Following this approach, psychologists have found that there are two major strategies popular with toddlers:

● **Referential techniques** These are words that refer to people, animals, and objects in the toddler's immediate surroundings. Each word refers to someone or something she sees regularly in her environment.

● **Expressive techniques** These are words that refer to actions people carry out or to interactions between people. Rather than focusing on particular objects or people, expressive words convey a sense of what is happening.

Psychologists studying the characteristics of children who use these different vocabulary strategies have found a number of features that distinguish the two groups. In general, children whose early words are mainly referential tend to use shorter sentences later on, although they often speak more clearly and find it easier to make themselves understood. Children whose first words are mainly expressive use voice tone, word accentuation, and other nonverbal techniques more effectively to convey meaning.

There is some evidence that a child's vocabulary strategy is influenced by her parents' linguistic style. For instance, one study found that mothers who tend to give more instructions and directions to their child (rather than descriptions of objects and people) usually have children who have a referential strategy. The same effect is found when mothers tend to name objects and people when talking to their child. However, as a child's language develops over the next year or so, she starts to use both styles anyway.

Above Naming objects with your child will help to broaden her vocabulary. Even though she may not use the words immediately, she will absorb their meaning.

16 – 18 months

THE MAIN CHANGES TO LOOK FOR:

● **Vocabulary** She steadily builds up her vocabulary, which includes nouns, pronouns, and even adjectives. You can reasonably expect her to use between ten and twenty words by the time she reaches 18 months. Bear in mind, however, that she understands a lot more words than she can say herself.

● **Listening skills** You'll find that she turns her head whenever she hears any noise. And if she can't actually see the source of the sound, she will probably try to find where it is, perhaps by toddling into the next room or by trying to peer out of the window to see what is going on outside. She identifies many of the sounds she hears.

● **Instructions** Now that she understands more spoken language than ever before, she is able to follow a very basic instruction that has only one piece of information. For instance, if she is asked to put the cup on the table, she carries out this request accurately as long as there are not too many other distractions.

● **Word combinations** Some children start to combine two words together to form a short phrase (although many children don't acquire this skill for another few months at least). She may say something like "juice gone" when she realizes her drink of orange juice is finished—and the phrase makes sense to you.

● **Songs** Instead of waiting for you to start singing, you might notice that when she plays quietly on her own she starts to sing to herself. You won't be able to make out the words, but you will probably be able to identify the particular song that she's trying to sing. She is very happy with her efforts.

Below **This little girl can now easily understand and act upon simple instructions like passing the cup to her friend.**

Wrong Words

Your child sometimes uses an inappropriate word to describe an object because she sees that the object shares a characteristic with something similar—for instance, she calls an elephant a "cat" because both animals have four legs. Sometimes she uses an inappropriate word because she can't think of the correct word and just wants to say something. And occasionally she gets genuinely confused, having misheard a word that you used earlier. Toddlers often laugh at the sounds of words they make up themselves. So when your child says one of her self-created words (that is, complete gibberish as far as you are concerned), she immediately howls with laughter. To you her word makes no sense at all, but to her it's the best joke ever.

Body Language
Extreme Gestures

As the steady growth of spoken vocabulary occurs, your toddler may go through a phase of overexaggerated body language, almost as if he thinks that you won't understand unless it is crystal clear. Every gesture becomes emphasized, and he may repeat his actions several times until he is satisfied that you fully grasp what he is trying to convey to you. This applies to both negative and positive emotions.

Above This little boy's enjoyment of the toy car is written all over his face and he is throwing his whole body into the action of driving.

For instance, his tantrums become more extreme when things don't go according to plan. He lies on the floor screaming louder than ever before, kicking his legs into the air and perhaps slapping his hands against the carpet. In previous months he may have sulked when you said "no" to him, but now he expresses his dismay using completely unambiguous body language. There is no doubt about the meaning of his actions.

Likewise, if you don't understand exactly what he is pointing to on the other side of the room, he doesn't waste any time dragging you over to it. He wants you to know his ideas and he'll do what he can to get the message across. The same applies to his positive emotions, too. He chuckles louder than ever before, and his smile seems to be broader. His gestures, facial expressions, and general mannerisms communicate his ideas and feelings very clearly. One explanation for this overzealous use of nonverbal communication is that his use of spoken language requires great effort. There will be many instances when you don't know what he is saying because his speech is unclear or he doesn't use a recognizable word. He expects to have to work hard to communicate with speech, and it's possible that he transfers this expectation to nonverbal communication, too—hence his exaggerated body language.

Below Because his mother has not understood that he needs help with a toy, this little boy takes it to her—a more immediate way of getting what he wants than using words.

84

16 – 18 months

DETERMINATION RULES

One of your toddler's most distinctive characteristics at this point is his unswerving determination to get what he wants. He does not tolerate anyone who stands in his way, and therefore confrontations are common. But most expressions of his determination are made nonverbally, not through his spoken language. There are typically four levels of body language used to convey this personality trait:

Right Although this little girl has understood her mother's instruction not to empty the bag of balls, she deliberately ignores her.

- **Passive nonemotional** Your toddler simply ignores what you say and continues as if he did not hear you. If told to stop playing with an object, he keeps on handling it. There is no change in his behavior or expression, because he intends to ignore you completely.

- **Passive emotional** At this level, your child still does not actively resist but you can see his underlying feelings. His facial expression tenses and his eyes narrow; his mouth muscles also tighten. Your toddler doesn't look at you, but you can tell that he is displeased.

- **Active nonemotional** When he asks for something that you refuse to give, he decides to reach for it anyway. The absence of any change in his facial expression, coupled with his unexpected action that goes against your instruction, means that you may be caught off-guard.

- **Active emotional** This level is reached when he explodes with rage. He is so determined to get his own way that his anger spills over uncontrollably. Tears flow, loud screams are heard, and in his tantrum he may try to hit you. Once you calm him, his body language tells you he is sorry.

The Importance of Touch

Your toddler has better control over his hand and body movements, enabling him to use touch more effectively. This most primitive and intimate form of nonverbal communication remains important for him. In later years he uses touch in a more exclusive manner, but for now it is one of his major channels of communication. For instance, he clings tightly to you when he is anxious or afraid—physical contact with you provides him with reassurance. He likes to climb up to sit on your knee when you read him a story because that makes the whole experience more pleasurable for him, and he tries to give you a kiss when you bring your cheek close to his face.

85

Top Tips to Help Your Child

Encourage Talking

- **Introduce pretend play to your toddler** This new form of play that emerges during this phase of development creates new opportunities for language stimulation. Set up her cuddly toys in a circle and pretend to talk to them. Do this with her a couple of times and you'll discover that she plays this game with her cuddly toys on her own.

- **Engage her attention** At this age she can be so engrossed in play that she doesn't hear what you say to her. To ensure your toddler listens to your words, make sure that she stops her current game to listen. Play activities will distract her attention away from you.

- **Read her stories** There is clear evidence from research that reading a story to your child for a few minutes each day will have a positive effect on her language skills. It helps to let her see the book and the pages as you turn them. Although she can't read, this allows her to see that reading follows a specific direction.

- **Play with a toy telephone** She watches you talk on the telephone and perhaps has spoken a couple of words when you held it to her mouth. Consequently she is enthusiastic about a toy telephone and has lots of imaginative conversations with her friends and relatives. You can pretend to talk to her on your own toy telephone.

- **Give her space and time** Although your toddler has plenty that she wants to say for herself, she needs time to organize her thoughts and words. This may not always be convenient for you. Do your best to avoid rushing her. If she senses your irritation, she'll become confused and unable to say what she wants.

- **Expand her understanding of the names of body parts** She is still too young to learn how to say the names of, for instance, her feet, hands, eyes, ears, and mouth, but she is able to extend her understanding of these words. In addition to the ones she already knows, point out one or two of her body parts whose names she isn't familiar with. This way she will steadily improve her understanding.

- **Don't correct words** Resist the temptation to correct your toddler when she uses wrong words. In most instances, these errors will spontaneously self-correct in the next few months anyway as her language skills consolidate and increase. Constant correction of these natural word errors could inhibit her speech development.

16 – 18 months

Use and Interpret Body Language

- **Provide social opportunities** More than ever now, she learns from being with other children her own age. She still plays alongside them, not with them, but she watches their every move and gesture. You may find that after a session at parent-and-toddler group she starts to imitate the gestures of a child who was there.

- **Make eye contact** Try to make good eye contact with your toddler during a conversation, because this encourages her to do the same (though don't stare at her). Eye contact is an important social skill, conveying a sense of interest and concern. It also increases the likelihood that the listener will pay attention to what is being said.

- **Don't overreact to exaggerated body language** Remember that her more flamboyant use of nonverbal communication during this period is connected with her desire to express herself. It doesn't mean her feelings are more intense now than they were previously. So try to react normally, not in an extreme manner.

- **Keep rules despite her protests** It's hard for you to maintain rules at home when your toddler has one of those raging tantrums that leave each of you shattered. The onslaught of her nonverbal barrage can be emotionally draining. Yet don't give in to this behavior; otherwise she'll learn that tantrums get her what she wants.

- **Use soothing gestures** She continues to respond to your body language. When you see that she is upset—even if this has arisen through a confrontation with you—use nonverbal soothing gestures to calm her. For instance, stroke her cheek softly with your fingers or gently stroke her hair. You don't need to speak at all; the gesture alone will be enough to relax her tension.

- **Permit choices** Your toddler is capable of communicating her desires through body language. If she pushes aside one toy you offered her to play with a different one, let her make that choice. This is part of the normal process through which your child starts to develop her individual personal identity.

- **When saying "no," use gestures, too** Your toddler won't like it when she can't get her own way and may try to make you change your mind. However, your refusal to give in to her demands will appear more decisive and emphatic when you accompany the spoken word with appropriate hand gestures and facial expressions.

Toys Cuddly toys and teddy bears that she can snuggle up to ● realistic toy telephone with ringing sounds ● plastic cups, saucers, and spoons ● range of storybooks with pictures ● lots of bath toys ● toy musical instruments ● inset boards with several wooden pieces ● shape sorter ● small wooden construction bricks ● large sand and water tray

87

Questions and Answers

Q My toddler usually walks away from a toy or game after a few minutes, without saying a word. Does this mean she is bored or that she has weak concentration?

A Her behavior could be a combination of boredom and weak concentration. Look at the toys she has, and note the toys she actually plays with. Perhaps she hasn't had any new toys for a while, or maybe she tends to play with the same few. If so, encourage variety in her play. Either arrange for her to have different toys or encourage her to play with other toys the next time. And when she does get up after a few minutes, gently suggest that she sit down again to play for a little longer.

Q When I take my 17-month-old to parent-and-toddler group he doesn't say a word; he just clings to me like a limpet. Should I push him away so that he is forced to cope more independently?

A His body language is telling you "I'm afraid of these other children and I want to stay beside you because that makes me feel safe." Put like that, the strategy of forcing him away from you probably won't work—it could make him feel even more miserable. Give him time to adjust to this new social context. Several visits may pass before he feels confident enough to leave your side, but his natural social instinct will take over eventually and he will gradually take a few hesitant steps away from you.

Q How can I encourage my toddler not to express his anger through hitting me or his sister? The moment his temper rises, his first reaction is to lash out without saying a word.

A Aggressive behavior of this sort is typical at this age, and stems from your toddler's lack of control over his emotions. Instead of voicing his feelings, he acts impulsively on them. Hence he hits his older sister or anyone else who happens to be in the immediate vicinity. Discourage this nonverbal aggression every time you see it. Let him know that you are displeased with his behavior and explain that it is not acceptable to hit someone. His sister should not be expected to tolerate it either. Continue to discourage his aggression using this strategy.

16 – 18 months

Q Is it too early to teach my toddler the names of colors? I know that she can't say the actual words, but I have a feeling that she recognizes some of the colors because she always picks pullovers that are red.

A Color naming doesn't occur until much later than color recognition, so you can't reasonably expect your toddler to name colors. But there is no harm in starting off the learning process by pointing out the basic colors at this stage, such as red, yellow, blue, and green. When dressing her with blue trousers, for instance, say to your toddler, "These are your blue pants," and show her another item that is the same color. Although she only looks and doesn't say anything in response, she probably takes in your comments.

Q I'm worried because my toddler talks to himself. When he plays on his own, I often hear him chatting as if there is someone else beside him. Is this sort of behavior normal?

A Psychologists call this form of language "self-directing speech," because it is your child's way of giving himself instructions. You probably do this as well, such as when you tell yourself to be brave as you visit the dentist or when you encourage yourself to run that extra few yards while out jogging. If you actually listen to the words your child uses, you'll realize that most of his talk when alone is of this nature. It is both normal and helpful for your child, and also gives him further opportunities to improve his speech.

Q My child is nearly 18 months and yet still prefers to point instead of speaking. What's the best way to discourage this habit? I know she can say the word.

A This is a habit, and like all habits it can be changed. There are two strategies you can use. First, don't respond to her pointing gesture, at least for a couple of seconds. You may find that when she realizes she doesn't get the desired response from you, she chooses to use the spoken word instead. Be careful not to ignore her for too long, however, or her frustration could build up. Second, say the name of the object that she points to, even though she knows this word already. This teaches her by example.

89

Development
16–18 Month Skills

MOVEMENT
- Walks unsteadily with support up and down stairs. Some toddlers may use different strategies such as crawling up the steps or going down on their bottom.
- Walks confidently about the home and outside.
- Picks up toys or other objects from the floor without toppling over.
- Trots toward you across the room, but may become unsteady if she starts to run.
- Starts to use climbing frames and other playground equipment, but will need constant supervision.
- May enjoy splashing and kicking in the swimming pool.

LANGUAGE
- Is able to follow and act on simple instructions.
- Consistently uses approximately seven or eight words, although her understanding extends to many more, and may reach the point of rapid vocabulary expansion.
- Combines language and gestures to express her needs.
- Starts to learn the names of different parts of the body.
- Enjoys songs and nursery rhymes and will perhaps join in with some sounds and actions.

SOCIAL AND EMOTIONAL
- May have a tantrum when she doesn't get her own way as she begins to assert her sense of independence.
- Wants to do more for herself, especially with feeding and dressing.
- Learns good eating habits by sharing mealtimes with others.
- Begins to learn basic social skills like passing a toy to another child.
- Plays alongside other children, watching them closely, and learns by taking in how they interact and play.

16 – 18 months

HAND–EYE COORDINATION
- Sees a connection between her hand movements and the effect they cause. For example, she pulls at a string that is attached to a toy to make it move toward her.
- Enjoys making random marks on paper, using crayons or paints.
- Starts to feed herself with her hands and a spoon.
- Holds two small items in each hand at the same time.
- May want to help dress herself.
- Hand preference may become apparent.
- Claps her hands together.
- Successfully completes a simple inset board activity.
- Leaves through a book, turning two or three pages at a time.

LEARNING
- Combines the use of different skills and capacities, such as concentration, memory, hand-eye control, and understanding, to complete a complex task such as a simple inset board.
- Solves simple problems like removing the lid from a box to see inside.
- Learns the basic concepts of quantities and volume through playing with water.
- Improved attention span enables her to concentrate on and complete more demanding activities and tasks.
- Understands and follows stories that are read to her and responds to familiar characters.
- Remembers where she put an item that she is interested in, such as a favorite toy.
- Will try to imitate your actions.

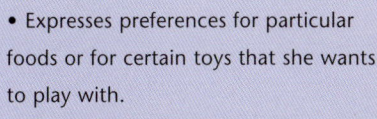

- Expresses preferences for particular foods or for certain toys that she wants to play with.
- May become jealous when you pay attention to others.
- May deliberately behave badly to get your attention.

91

19–21 Months

Three major changes occur in your child's spoken language around this time. First, he experiences a "vocabulary explosion," in which the range of single words he speaks rapidly increases. Second, he begins to combine two words together to form phrases or short sentences that have a clear and distinctive meaning. Lastly, your toddler realizes that spoken language is an effective way of making social contact with other people and his interest in conversations increases. His use of language, therefore, becomes more dynamic and purposeful. His use of body language is more subtle and he uses clusters of gestures more effectively to express his feelings.

Language Development
Words and Phrases

Most of the new spoken words that your child acquires during this period are naming words, referring to objects, animals, or people. It's almost as if she suddenly gains insight into language, and realizes that words can be used to apply to everything she sees. This gives her the confidence to experiment with spoken language. You find that she tries to give a name to all objects and people. She is not bothered by her mistakes—she simply enjoys talking!

Above You will notice how much more your child participates when looking at picture books, very often taking the lead in pointing out and naming objects and characters.

Your toddler's words at this stage are often "overextensions," which is the hallmark of her early vocabulary. This means she frequently uses words to refer to a larger category of objects than you do. Take the word "mama," for instance. She applies this word to you when she sees you or wants to attract your attention, and this has special meaning for both of you. Yet you may find that she uses the word "mama" to refer to other women, too.

Don't be disappointed when she does this, however, because it does not indicate that she thinks you are the same as any other woman she sees—she knows exactly who you are. It's just that in this early stage of language development, her limited vocabulary, coupled with her developing understanding of the world, results in this tendency to overextend the meaning of words to objects or people that are similar in some ways, even though she fully understands that they are different.

Her first two-word phrase—which should be regarded as her form of a sentence—appears and is very basic. She might say "want milk" or "dada car," for example. These early phrases usually include nouns, verbs, and adjectives, but little else. This represents a huge step forward for your toddler as she starts to use language more creatively.

19 – 21 months

THE MAIN CHANGES TO LOOK FOR:

● **Vocabulary** Her range of individual spoken words begins to increase at an accelerating rate. It may have taken her the past three months to go from one to seven words, but by the end of this next three-month period she can use at least fifty different words. She likes to talk about everything in her immediate surroundings, using language at every opportunity.

● **Meaningful phrases** Her two-word combinations carry specific meaning, which may not always be clear to you. For instance, "dada car" might mean "I can hear dad's car outside" or "I would like to see dad's car" or "Where is dad's car?" She desperately wants to communicate and becomes annoyed when you don't understand what she says.

● **Creativity** One of the remarkable features of your child's language at this stage is that she often uses phrases she has never heard before, such as "all gone juice." The appearance of new structures and phrases like this confirm the dynamic, creative nature of her language skills now; she applies linguistic rules to make new words.

● **Picture identification** A favorite activity at this stage is to sit beside you as you slowly turn the pages of her picture book. No longer content to be passive as you read to her, she now leans forward, peers carefully at each page, points to the picture, and names the objects contained in it. And she probably gets many of them right.

● **Conversations** Whereas previously your toddler blurted out her words the moment she thought of them, she now shows greater awareness of and interest in two-way conversations. She makes more of an effort to listen while you speak, and replies after a short pause. There are greater attempts to synchronize her speech with yours.

Pronunciation

Your toddler's pronunciation of letters and words is still evolving at this stage, making many of her words unclear at first. She uses more consonants now, particularly those involving the muscles at the front of her mouth such as "b," "p," "f," and "m," and most of the vowel sounds, too. You'll gradually gain recognition of her sound patterns, though adults who don't know her well may struggle to understand what she says until they get used to her particular speech characteristics. She may not be able to make sounds such as "r" and "k" (because they involve a complex use of muscles toward the back of her mouth), but she can hear the difference when someone else uses them at the start of words.

Left By 20 months or so children develop real conversational ability in the way that they are able to listen, take in information, and respond to others.

95

Body Language Combinations

With increased control over his body, limb, and face movements, your child is more able to communicate nonverbally using more than one channel at a time. Instead of using, say, facial expression alone to express emotions, without deliberate intention he now combines this with body posture, breathing, eye movements, and other dimensions of body language. It takes only a slight difference in these combinations of gestures to convey a totally different meaning.

Here are a couple of typical messages your child expresses at this age and the body language associated with each of them:

- **"I don't know this person and I'm shy."** It is common for a toddler to become self-conscious in the presence of someone he doesn't know very well, even though he is generally confident with people. The following body language combinations indicate shyness: he looks down at his feet to avoid making eye contact, he holds your hand tightly and presses himself into your side, his face grows a deeper shade of red the longer he remains in that situation, and he may even put his hands over his eyes to physically block out the other person.

- **"I'm unhappy and I feel thoroughly miserable."** Of course there are moments of temporary unhappiness during the toddler years, though these soon pass. They are not always obvious, however. The following body language combinations indicate unhappiness: his shoulders lose their natural tension and become floppy; he loses his interest in toys and his body movements are generally lethargic; he seems to have a greater than usual need for hugs, cuddles, and reassurances from you; and he becomes unexpectedly quiet or withdrawn.

Below **Constant demands for hugs are a sign that your child is not entirely happy. Children often go through phases of being clingy, though these usually pass quickly.**

SILENCE

Your toddler increasingly uses spoken language to take part in a conversation, and he soon learns that to have any form of discussion with another person, he needs to say nothing at some point so that the other person has a chance to speak. The notion of speaking, then listening, then speaking, in a reciprocal relationship with someone else, introduces him to the concept of silence. He realizes that the absence of spoken words is a powerful form of communication.

One of the most effective ways for your child to express his anger nonverbally—assuming he doesn't have a raging tantrum—is to say absolutely nothing when you speak to him.

Ignoring your questions or comments tells you immediately that something is troubling him, and the look of anger on his face confirms that that is exactly what he feels.

19 – 21 months

Above This little girl's silence is a sign that she is utterly absorbed in looking at her book and requires all her concentration for this activity.

It's Your Turn Now

Conversational skills are complex, because the speaker has to indicate clearly that the other person can stop listening now, that it is that person's turn to talk. Subtle nonverbal signals used by a speaker to let the listener know it is permissible to speak typically include dropping the voice pitch, stopping the hand gestures that accompany speech, and lowering the voice volume.

When your toddler is aged between 19 and 21 months, however, he is not aware of these nonverbal signs that invite him to take his turn, so he frequently interrupts before you have finished. It's not that he is rude or forceful, it's that he genuinely fails to recognize the appropriate moment for him to speak. This awareness improves with experience.

Other emotions can be expressed by total silence, too. In fact, results from research studies suggest that in addition to representing anger, silence can be used to indicate a child's sense of complete boredom, of anxiety or fear, and of disdain.

Of course, your toddler's silence can also be a sign that he is perfectly happy with his current activity or that he is concentrating hard on something—or even that he is fast asleep! But if his silence isn't appropriate to the context—for instance, if he says absolutely nothing when with his friends, or if he is totally silent when he is with you on a shopping trip—then consider the possibility that his silence means he is unsettled about something. It's important to respond to your child's body language, not just to the words he says to you.

Nonverbal communication usually happens without any thought behind it and is less controlled and therefore more genuine than verbal communication. And when you find that you have interpreted his body language accurately—for instance, he was much happier after you cuddled him, even though he had not complained to you—this gives you increased confidence in your own ability to respond to your child's needs. It also increases his trust in you as a caring, loving parent. Remember that in addition to tuning in to his nonverbal communication, you can do a lot to encourage him to use it more effectively.

97

Top Tips to Help Your Child

Encourage Talking

- **Use current experiences** Your toddler's memory is short, which means she may forget something that happened earlier in the day. So encourage her to talk about her experiences as they occur. For instance, she can tell you about the toy she is playing with, about the food she is eating, and about the clothes with which you are dressing her right now.

- **Expect quiet times** No matter how much your toddler likes to chat to you, there will be times when she just wants to sit quietly, without saying a word. That's fine and is nothing to worry about. When she is ready to start talking again she will make comments, but in the meantime allow her to say little or nothing at all.

- **Praise her when she talks to others** Her sociability varies greatly. When you do see her make an effort to chat to someone other than yourself—perhaps to your friend's child who visits or to the checkout clerk at the supermarket—tell her how pleased you are that she was so talkative. She responds positively to your praise and approval.

- **Name objects and people** Most of her words at this stage refer to these anyway. You can help her, however, by naming objects that she sees. Don't just point to the item and say the appropriate word; instead, use the item's name in a sentence, whether in question form or statement form. She'll pick out the word that refers to the object.

- **Compile more complex listening games** Make up more games that involve her in listening for sounds. Now that she's a little older you can make the listening challenge more demanding—for instance, by asking her to identify sounds that she isn't so familiar with, such as a key turning in a lock or water pouring out of a bottle into a cup.

- **Play music and sing songs** She is more able to sing along to the words of her favorite songs, particularly if you join in, too. When listening to a children's tune, you may find that she tries to make up her own words to accompany it. Let her sing whatever words she wants—this helps her practice old and new sound combinations.

- **Use "third-party" instructions** You know that she follows basic instructions given to her. Now you can extend this by giving her instructions that involve someone else. For instance, suggest that she give the cup to her doll, or that she take the book to her teddy bear. This task is more demanding; she needs to listen, interpret, and then carry it out.

19 – 21 months

Use and Interpret Body Language

- **Check out her silences** Try to ascertain the meaning of her silence. Bear in mind that there can be lots of different reasons for her to become quiet, and they are not all negative. Study other aspects of her body language, too, before reaching a firm interpretation. You may find that what you thought was her anger is nothing more than her concentration.

- **Don't jump to conclusions** Because you know your toddler's moods and have become very familiar with her body language, it's easy to assume that you understand exactly what her body language means. But she's constantly changing at the moment, and she finds new ways to express herself nonverbally. Yesterday's gesture might have a different meaning today.

- **Accompany spoken language with gestures** Her understanding is enhanced when you explain something using spoken language that is accompanied by appropriate nonverbal gestures. For instance, you could describe a big round ball and while saying these words use your hands to mime a large round shape. This helps her grasp the meaning of what you say to her.

- **Exaggerate pauses in conversation** You can help her learn the social rules of conversation by making longer pauses before speaking. Just wait an extra second or two before taking your turn in the discussion. This technique slows down the whole pace of the conversation, ensuring that she doesn't rush through it and making her more aware of the breaks in speech.

- **Mirror her body language** Smile when she smiles, laugh when she laughs, and frown when she frowns. This is not mimicry or imitation; rather it is your way of demonstrating that you understand what she feels. It's a form of empathy. Your toddler is more likely to continue using body language when she knows it is an effective form of communication.

- **Expect episodes of shyness** Your toddler may be lively for most of the time, but there will almost certainly be moments when her body language indicates she is experiencing a bout of shyness. Such behavior is normal during this period of development. Give her a gentle cuddle and wait with her as her social confidence gradually returns.

- **Use listening gestures** Your toddler starts to pick up nonverbal social skills from you, which can help her form relationships with others later on. When she talks to you, use facial and head gestures that show you are listening (for example, nod your head slowly, frown slightly to show you are concentrating, tilt your head slightly). She'll copy these gestures.

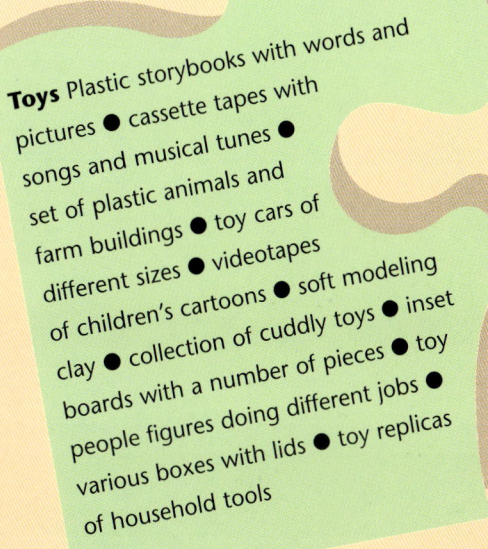

Toys Plastic storybooks with words and pictures ● cassette tapes with songs and musical tunes ● set of plastic animals and farm buildings ● toy cars of different sizes ● videotapes of children's cartoons ● soft modeling clay ● collection of cuddly toys ● inset boards with a number of pieces ● toy people figures doing different jobs ● various boxes with lids ● toy replicas of household tools

99

Questions and Answers

Q A couple of days ago my toddler stuck her tongue out at someone and that person laughed because they thought it was funny. Since then she sticks her tongue out at everybody. This is embarrassing. What should I do?

A The positive reaction from the person who laughed at her tongue-thrusting antics has reinforced her behavior, so she repeats it in the expectation of receiving the same response from everyone else. She is too young to realize that this gesture is socially inappropriate. When she sticks her tongue out at you, neither laugh nor make a big fuss; instead, frown at her and turn away. Do this consistently and within a couple of days your toddler will no longer stick her tongue out so frequently.

Q My toddler is 21 months old and is a good speaker. Yet he mixes up letters, and sometimes even complete syllables get put in the wrong order. Is this difficulty normal or is there something wrong with him?

A Individual letters and words vary in difficulty of pronunciation, so it's only natural that your toddler occasionally makes minor errors like this when learning to talk. This is part and parcel of the learning process. Instead of drawing attention to them, respond to the sounds and words you know he intended to say. You'll find that his speech spontaneously improves with maturity and that this pattern of noticeable minor errors greatly diminishes.

Q What should I do to encourage better behavior when my child is with others? At parent-and-toddler group, she is very forceful. When she wants a toy, she stands close to the other child and has a threatening expression.

A She uses this form of body language because it works. In most instances, a threatening toddler gets her own way with others her age. However, none of her peers will want to play with her. When you see her do this, intervene by bringing her away from the other child. Tell her to leave that toddler alone and to wait until the toy is available. Calm her if she becomes angry with you. Of course she won't like this, but she'll slowly learn that her behavior is unacceptable.

19 – 21 months

Q My child has learned to say the word "no" and uses this all the time now. He genuinely expects me to do what he says. How can I change this?

A Like all toddlers, he is full of his own self-importance. He wants to be the boss, the person in charge at home, and having heard you use the word "no" to stop him from doing something, he thinks this is a great idea. At this age, he truly assumes you will respond to his negative command and may become furious when you don't. The best strategy at this stage is to ignore him when he speaks like that to you; once he realizes that "no" isn't working the way he wants, he'll stop using it so frequently.

Q I notice that my toddler's speech becomes unclear when he is excited. He seems to rush his words as though he is worried he'll forget what he wants to say. What should I do?

A This is a common problem with young children. His desire to speak to you is so overwhelming that he loses concentration, his words lose clarity, and he becomes more difficult to understand. When he starts to talk like this, try to slow his speech down by reacting calmly, by listening, and by speaking slowly to him in response. Don't get irritated with him or he may decide to stop telling you things altogether. You will find that your relaxed listening approach encourages him to relax when talking, and that his speech becomes clearer.

Q How can I encourage my child to make better eye contact with me? She has never been particularly good at this and tends to look away from me when we talk.

A Improving eye contact at this age is difficult, because it's hard to explain to a toddler about the significance of this gesture. In addition, you simply cannot force her to look at you when you speak to her. The more you try, the less likely she is to conform to your demand and you'll only end up fighting with her. However, when playing with her or talking to her, position yourselves so that she sits facing you instead of sitting side by side. This provides more opportunity for your toddler to look into your face while communicating.

Development

19–21 Month Skills

MOVEMENT
- Can undertake another activity while moving. For example, she can trail a pull-along toy behind her as she walks.
- Likes to climb over furniture.
- Can walk backward a few steps.
- Climbs up and down from a chair.
- Improved balance and coordination leads to fewer instances of tripping over and unexpected falls when she is walking and running.
- Is able to use a wider range of playground equipment. 
- Enjoys running freely in a park and in the garden.
- Walks upstairs with both feet on each step and without support.
- Can stop quickly when walking and can turn corners.

LANGUAGE
- Has extended her vocabulary to dozens of words, mostly nouns that describe a general class of object, such as "car" for all vehicles or "house" for all buildings.
- Tries to join in songs.
- Is interested in conversations and begins to learn conversational conventions, such as giving and waiting for answers.
- Puts words together to form two-word phrases. 
- Develops an understanding that speech is about social contact as well as communicating basic needs.
- Spots familiar characters and objects in picture books and photographs and tries to name them.
- Is clearer when asking for something that she wants: food, drink, or toys.

SOCIAL AND EMOTIONAL
- Appreciates your company and makes an effort to engage your attention through either talk or play.
- Shows that she is nearly ready to begin potty training, although full control is unlikely at this age.
- Persists in challenging decisions that she disagrees with.
- Begins to interact with other children but needs lots of basic social guidance.
- Is able to understand simple rules, although she may not always comply with them.
- Enjoys the security of a regular daily routine.
- May use attention-seeking devices such as grabbing your arm, and will often refuse to cooperate.

19 – 21 months

HAND–EYE COORDINATION
- Enjoys playing with modeling materials like play dough or clay, and sand and water, making shapes and drawing "pictures" into the surface.
- Likes rolling, throwing, and perhaps even catching balls, both large and small, though she will find large ones easier to grasp.
- Stacks small wooden blocks on top of each other to make a tower of perhaps five bricks.
- Pours water accurately from one container into another one without too much splashing.
- Makes increasingly deliberate marks on paper with a crayon.
- Can turn two to three pages of a book over at one time.
- Can use a cup without spilling its contents.

LEARNING
- Begins to use toys for imaginative play, as a result of her developing capacity for symbolic thought.
- Her increasing problem-solving ability enables her to complete an inset board with several pieces, and these toys are now well within her capability.
- Her developing curiosity makes her want to see what goes on outside and to explore closed cupboards.
- Uses all her senses, including sight, hearing, and touch, to learn about the world in which she lives, and becomes more confident in exploring new environments.
- Becomes more focused and determined and is more motivated to complete a challenging task.

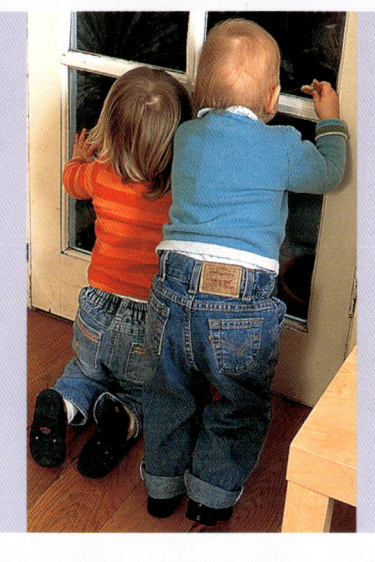

22–24 Months

Approaching the end of his second year, your toddler uses speech more effectively to communicate his needs, ideas, and feelings. There are clear signs that he understands basic grammatical rules, and his sentences follow a recognizable structure and format. He loves chatting to you, whether you feel like listening or not, and at moments you may long for earlier times when he had much less to say for himself! Your toddler also tries to talk to others his own age. The nonverbal communication of your 2-year-old is more assertive, more confident—he knows what he wants, and that is reflected in his body language.

Language Development
Telegraphic Speech

Your child's phrases contain two, three, or more words, and they now all follow a basic grammatical structure. Of course, her grammar is unsophisticated and yet she is able to convey meaning with reasonable accuracy. For instance, when she says, "want milk," you know she means, "I would like to have a drink of milk."

Perhaps the most noticeable characteristic of this early grammar, which develops around the age of 24 months, is that it lacks "inflections": in other words, it doesn't have the features that you would expect an adult to use. For instance, your toddler doesn't use plurals, nor does she use past or future tenses, prepositions, identifiers such as "the" and "a," or "ing" at the end of a verb. Later on she will, but for the time being these more mature speech dimensions are absent.

Studies have shown that if a child this age is asked simply to repeat a sentence such as "I would like to have a cookie," she automatically transforms it into her own grammar and replies along the lines of "want cookie." Known as telegraphic speech—because it resembles the type of language structure you would use when sending a telegram—this grammatical structure is neat, economical, and precise, and relies heavily on the use of nouns and verbs. Despite the omissions of the other key words, the meaning of her sentences is usually very clear to you.

Another characteristic of your toddler's speech at this age is that the order of words is nearly always appropriate. For instance, she is more likely to say "want ball" than to say "ball want." Appropriate word order is usually maintained even when she says things she hasn't heard you say before, suggesting she has built-in sensitivity to word order rather than just imitating phrases she has heard you use.

Above Pointing to and naming different parts of the body is great fun for this little girl, and she now takes on new words at a rapid rate.

106

22 – 24 months

THE MAIN CHANGES TO LOOK FOR:

- **Vocabulary** Don't bother trying to count the number of spoken words your toddler uses. Estimates suggest that the typical child of 24 months has a basic vocabulary of at least 100 words. New words appear each day, perhaps surprising you with the range. Your toddler loves the sounds of these words and they also enable her to speak to you more accurately, so that you have less difficulty understanding what she tells you.

- **Self-referring speech** Her increasing self-awareness results in her ability to connect spoken language with herself. And it's not just that she likes to use the word "me"—although this figures highly in her sentences—but that she is also able to identify some of her body parts. Ask your toddler "Where are your feet?" and watch as she points toward the right body part. She can point to her eyes, ears, nose, and mouth as well.

- **Object naming** Not only can she name specific objects in her daily environment when she wants to refer to them, but she can also accurately name them when asked. For instance, she doesn't use the word "cat" to describe every four-legged animal, and instead uses a different word for a dog and for a cat. It won't always sound exactly right, but her word does match the real word to a large extent.

Above In addition to naming a wide range of things in his books, this little boy now has a better understanding of the progression of a story.

- **Linguistic curiosity** Your toddler's fascination with other people's language intensifies. You'll probably find that she watches when you have a conversation with someone else, listening intently even though you know she cannot possibly understand every word she hears in that situation. It's almost as though she is trying to learn ways of improving her own language usage through studying and examining other people when they talk.

Frustration

You'd think that by now her frustrations would ease, and that those earlier outbursts when she couldn't make herself understood to you would disappear. After all, her new levels of vocabulary and grammar offer her an infinite number of ways to express herself. But it doesn't happen that way—if anything, your toddler's frustration actually increases. This occurs because changes in her language ability coincide with other developmental changes, such as her need to become more independent, to have a better understanding of the world around her, and to establish herself with other children. The growth in those personal needs outstrips her ability to express them verbally. She still wants to say more than her linguistic skills allow, and hence frustration remains.

Body Language
Confidence

Your toddler experiences a number of developmental changes as he nears his second birthday, resulting in a huge boost to his self-confidence. He feels more self-assured, more willing to take on new challenges, and more willing to express his thoughts and feelings. This is a time in his life when his belief in himself and his own abilities really takes off.

The developmental changes that underpin this surge in self-confidence include the following:

- **Mobility** He can move around independently without relying on you for support, and falls become less frequent.

- **Potty training** Most parents have started to potty train their child by this time, and have achieved some success in this already.

Below Friendships with other children now become established, and learning to share and take turns is an important part of this.

- **Speech** Your child's improved language skills afford him greater opportunity to express his inner feelings using words.

- **Friendships** Through attendance at parent-and-toddler group or nursery, he realizes that other children like him and want to be with him.

Left Success in potty training will give your child a real sense of achievement and independence and is a major step forward.

Below The ability to achieve more complicated tasks, like building a brick tower, involves balance and coordination and will increase your child's physical confidence.

22 – 24 months

This greater level of confidence shows through in your 2-year-old's body language. His back is held straighter when he walks, his shoulders are held back, and he tends to look straight ahead as he walks. Everything about his body and head movements tells you "I can do it. I feel good."

Confident body language of this sort, however, can land your toddler in difficult situations. For example, the gaze of a 2-year-old is so positive and fixed ahead when he walks that he doesn't see potential hazards lying at ground level—and hence he stumbles over low tables, stools, and large toys that he doesn't see lying on the floor. Similarly, his confident body language may be misinterpreted as recklessness or even downright disobedience—like the time he silently marched out the back door of your house when you weren't looking. He didn't deliberately break your house rules; he just believes that he can do anything and that nothing can harm him.

LOVING TOUCH DECLINES

Findings from psychological research reveal that although gentle touch between parent and baby is frequent in the early months of life—and in fact, a baby denied loving physical contact at that stage probably becomes anxious and unsettled—it tails off toward the end of the second year. There are developmental reasons for this. First, your toddler's independence means that you don't have to hold him when feeding, and you don't have to carry him everywhere. Second, he is now able to exercise choice about cuddling—he moves away from you if he doesn't want a hug at that moment.

On the other hand, the reduction of touch as a spontaneous form of nonverbal communication actually increases its emotional significance for your toddler. Since cuddles, hugs, and other loving gestures are no longer an essential part of your child's life, they are even more special now when they do occur. Stroking his face gently, for instance, when he plays peacefully with his toys for a while makes him beam with delight—he doesn't take these gestures for granted. And the same applies to his touch toward you, too.

The decline in the frequency of loving touch coincides with an increase in the frequency of hostile touch. More than ever before, your toddler is likely to express his anger, aggression, and self-interest through threatening physical gestures involving touch, such as hitting, pushing, snatching, and sometimes biting. Many parents are surprised at the ferocity of their child's body language when he has a tantrum; he seems so powerful and he can hurt others when angry.

Aggressive attention-seeking devices always call for an immediate response. Try to avoid confronting the situation head-on. Instead, divert your toddler's attention before her frustration erupts.

Tongue Projection

You may notice that when he concentrates on completing an activity such as a small jigsaw puzzle or making something with his building blocks, your toddler lets his mouth hang open and projects his tongue forward. He doesn't need to say a word—you know by his tongue and mouth positioning that his level of concentration is high. He might also do this when attempting to walk steadily across the room or when trying to keep his balance. Although tongue projection gives him a rather strange appearance, this gesture seems to be a natural form of self-guidance, a nonverbal way of reminding him to persevere without flinching. Psychologists are unable to say why this gesture has such importance for a child who concentrates.

Top Tips to Help Your Child

Encourage Talking

● **Involve her in mealtime discussions** Your toddler benefits from taking part in conversations during the family meal, just like everybody else. Of course, her news is probably less exciting (though not to her) than the stories of her older brothers and sisters, but give her the chance to speak anyway. Let her have her say. Through such opportunities she gains competence in self-expression.

● **Treat your toddler seriously** Let her see you listen to her remarks. Make good eye contact with her during her comments and nod or shake your head appropriately to confirm that she has your full attention. Her account might seem humorous to you, even though she is perfectly serious about what she says. Try to match your mood to hers.

● **Use varied spoken language** Your toddler partly models her language on the words she hears you use, so variety in your own speech is important, too. Use alternative words to express the same concept: for instance, "large" instead of "big," "tasty" instead of "nice," or "thrilled" instead of "happy." She'll instinctively incorporate these words into her own vocabulary.

● **Expect speech mistakes** She still has a lot to learn about spoken language, and making mistakes is part of the learning process. Don't worry about these minor errors, such as mispronunciations, words you can't clearly understand, or mix-ups in grammar—these will disappear spontaneously without any correction from you. She may continue to mix real-world and baby talk, even at this age.

● **Calm her when excited** You may find that your toddler's speech deteriorates when she becomes excited or agitated. In an excited state, the chances are her words lose clarity, they sound jumbled, and her vocabulary may be very restricted. At such times, do your best to calm your child. Once she settles down and regains control of her emotions, her speech will quickly improve.

● **Encourage lip and tongue movements** She enjoys wiggling her tongue, making strange sounds, and blowing saliva bubbles. Although you may find these habits irritating, they are good for her speech development! Suggest that she blow bubbles into a bowl of water using a straw, or that she makes the "b" sound repetitively. Lip games like these are fun and useful at the same time.

● **Deliberately modify a familiar story** Select one of her favorite stories, one that she knows thoroughly from start to finish. Then amend the story slightly, perhaps changing the name of a central character or adding a new piece of action that isn't in the original version. When reading this revised version to your child, watch for her reaction when she hears the changes.

22 – 24 months

Use and Interpret Body Language

- **Teach her calming techniques** As an adult, you use aspects of physical movement to relax yourself, perhaps breathing deeply when you feel tense or deliberately unclenching your fist when you are agitated. Explain to her that, for instance, she should let her arms hang loosely by her side when she feels angry or that she should relax her brow when feeling worried.

- **Make her aware of her facial expressions** Two-year-olds are very unaware of the effect that their facial appearance has on other people. Increase her sensitivity through statements like "You look so much nicer when you smile" or "People will think you are angry when you frown like that." This helps your toddler learn to modify and monitor her body language.

- **Don't make fun of her** At times her body language is so extreme that you may be tempted to laugh, such as when her lower lip forms an obvious pout or when she tries to outstare you in anger. Suppress your amusement, because it will only make her worse. Remember that she doesn't have full control over her nonverbal communication.

- **Encourage social gestures** Now is a good time for your 2-year-old to learn nonverbal social skills that can have a positive influence on the way she forms relationships with her peers. Take sharing, for example. If your child gives another child the opportunity to play with her toy—perhaps by handing it to her—she will make friends with greater ease.

- **Keep a close watch over her** More than ever before, your toddler expresses her needs through body movements. Her curiosity takes on a new lease on life and she likes to wander everywhere—you can't afford to take your eyes off her for a moment. Be prepared to set limits on how far she is allowed to roam, despite her resistance.

- **Continue to use touch** Although there may be a reduction in the amount of physical contact between you and your toddler, you'll both gain from maintaining appropriate loving touch in your relationship. Cuddles and all other suitable forms of body contact help keep your emotional connection strong. Boys needs this nonverbal communication just as much as girls, to express and receive positive feelings.

- **Reprimand for negative touch** Your toddler needs you to advise her on suitable behavior, so always discourage her negative use of touch, such as punching, slapping, and kicking. This nonverbal behavior is unacceptable in all instances. Tell her that she is not allowed to express her anger nonverbally like this toward another child or adult. Repeat the message when necessary.

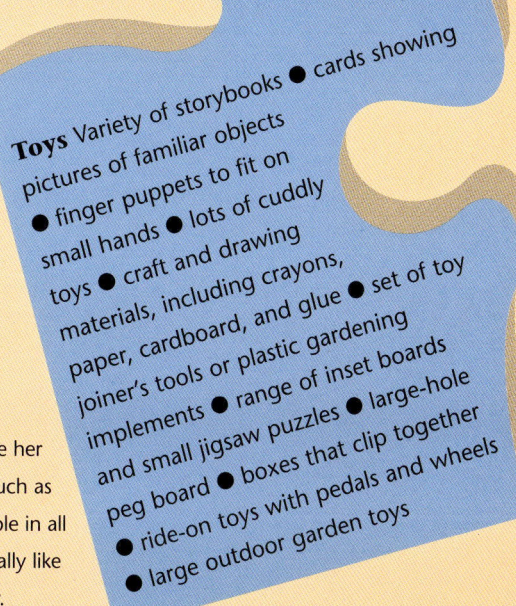

Toys Variety of storybooks ● cards showing pictures of familiar objects ● finger puppets to fit on small hands ● lots of cuddly toys ● craft and drawing materials, including crayons, paper, cardboard, and glue ● set of toy joiner's tools or plastic gardening implements ● range of inset boards and small jigsaw puzzles ● large-hole peg board ● boxes that clip together ● ride-on toys with pedals and wheels ● large outdoor garden toys

111

Questions and Answers

Q Should my child be able to understand my body language by now? Even when he sees me scowl at his behavior, he smiles at me and continues misbehaving.

A It is likely that your toddler interprets your nonverbal communication very well, but chooses to ignore it because he wants to continue with his current activity! At this age, he realizes immediately that the look on your face indicates disapproval. In his attempt to change your opinion, he throws you a huge smile and does not alter his behavior, in the hope that this will be acceptable to you. Instead of relying on facial expression alone, couple your frown with a clear verbal statement about your disapproval of his actions. That way he will understand your meaning for sure.

Q What can I do to stop my 2-year-old's stuttering? I find that he does this a lot at the moment.

A Many children this age develop a stutter, almost as though they try to say too much too quickly and end up confused. Yours probably says the initial letter of the word, then simply repeats it several times before completing the word; or maybe he repeats the whole word over and over again. Don't worry—this type of speech difficulty usually passes spontaneously. When he does stutter like this, resist the temptation to guess the word for him. Instead, stay calm, appear relaxed, and give him time to finish what he wants to say. If he suspects you are impatient or annoyed, his stutter may actually increase.

Q During mealtimes our child, who is 23 months old, flicks his food across the table. Sometimes it lands on me or on his older sister, and inevitably a fight breaks out. How can I stop this habit?

A Step back and look at the mealtime situation objectively in order to understand the meaning of this disruptive nonverbal behavior. The most likely explanation is that your toddler flicks his food in an attempt to make himself the center of attention. Consider that possibility. If you think this may be the reason, change the situation so that he can achieve his goal in other ways. For instance, make a point of talking to him before he starts to flick his food, or ask him questions during the meal.

22 – 24 months

Q Is it okay for my toddler to make up his own songs, or is it better for him to learn songs that everyone else already knows?

A What matters above all else is that your growing child uses spoken language in a variety of formats. Bear in mind that he likes words and he enjoys playing with speech by devising his own songs. The advantage of this is that he doesn't need to follow a script; he sings any words that come into his head. On the downside, nobody else can join in with him because only he knows the words. That's why you should certainly let him create his own lyrics when he wants to, but teach him songs that other children and adults know, too.

Q Sometimes when I read my toddler an exciting story he bursts into tears and seems frightened by it. Is this normal?

A Yes. He is just as likely to experience fear as you are, perhaps more so because he has difficulty separating fact from fiction. As he listens, he becomes totally engrossed by the words and their meaning, especially if you read using a dramatic voice tone. And if you make it scary by, say, lowering your voice at moments of tension or shrieking at dramatic points in the story, then your toddler is so involved that your behavior makes him really afraid. If you recognize when this happens, then just use a lighter tone of voice and monitor your toddler's reaction very carefully.

Q I have noticed that my toddler gets very upset whenever I criticize her. Should I never tell her that she is naughty?

A There is a difference between criticizing your toddler (for instance, "You are a naughty girl for doing that") and criticizing her actions ("What you did was naughty"). This is a subtle but important difference in the way you use words to convey disapproval, and your toddler will be sensitive to it. That's why it's best to offer criticism positively. For instance, instead of saying "You're naughty for deliberately splashing paint on the wall," you could say "You're usually so well behaved and that's why I'm surprised you deliberately splashed paint on the wall." The latter wording expresses disapproval while reassuring your toddler that you still love her.

113

Development

22–24 Month Skills

MOVEMENT
- Pushes a pedal toy along with her feet, although she probably cannot yet turn the pedals.
- Can stand on one foot while using the other to kick a ball.
- Runs confidently and rarely falls, although this activity still requires quite a lot of concentration.
- Moves fast as long as she goes in a straight line.
- Is unable to stop quickly when running.
- Is able to throw and catch a ball from a sitting position.
- Enjoys dancing to music because she now has more rhythm.
- Balance has improved so she can squat with ease.
- Can adjust her balance well on a swing.

LANGUAGE
- Accurately identifies everyday objects placed in front of her.
- Experiments with different (perhaps "incorrect") word combinations.
- Tackles most sounds but often mixes up or mispronounces certain consonants such as "c" or "s."
- Names the main parts of her body.
- Listens with interest to other people talking to each other.
- Her vocabulary is at least 200 words, often combined in short sentences.

LEARNING
- Understands that she can manipulate objects to learn more about them. For example, she twists objects to see inside them.
- Is enthusiastic about imaginative play, creating stories and scenes using toys, such as figures, to act them out.
- Watches you closely, then copies you as a way of learning new skills.
- Has an unquenchable thirst for information and asks lots of questions about everything around her.
- Is increasingly able to understand the explanations given to her.
- Will be able to remember and recount some past events.
- Is able to find a toy that she has played with previously.

22 – 24 months

HAND–EYE COORDINATION
- Looks at books for several minutes, studying each picture, pointing to images that catch her interest, and turning the pages.
- Can participate increasingly in helping to dress and undress herself.
- Combines her index finger and thumb effectively in the pincer grip to pick up small objects.
- Receives and passes objects from your hand to hers and back again.
- Makes increasingly rhythmic sounds with simple musical instruments such as drums and tambourines.

SOCIAL AND EMOTIONAL
- Enjoys the company of other children, but has trouble sharing her toys and doesn't play cooperatively.
- Is able to feed herself with a spoon effectively.
- Potty training is probably under way, but her bladder and bowel control may not yet be totally reliable.
- Wants to help wash herself at bathtime and brush her teeth.
- Enjoys the responsibility of carrying out small tasks.
- May cry when separated from you temporarily, although she soon stops when you are out of sight.
- May be shy with strangers.

25–30 Months

The change in your child's language is noticeable as he expands his vocabulary to include more nouns, pronouns, adjectives, and prepositions. In this sense, his spoken language becomes more mature. Conversations continue to fascinate him and he likes to talk, initiating verbal interactions more readily. This is the stage when he begins to ask question after question in his search for increased knowledge. Your child's improving memory enables him to refer to previous experiences when talking to you. During his third year, his nonverbal communication becomes far more sophisticated and complex, and has many of the characteristics of adult body language.

Language Development
Grammatical Rules and Pronouns

Your child's grammatical understanding improves, but it still retains some immature features. One characteristic of speech at this age—overregularization—has attracted considerable attention from psychologists. This occurs when your child applies a regular rule to an irregular word—for instance, when she says "me doed this" (using the word "doed" instead of "did") or when she says "me drinkded milk" (using the word "drinkded" instead of "drank"). This linguistic phenomenon may start to appear in your child's speech between 25 and 30 months.

It's as if your child learns the regular rule that she should add "ed" to the end of a word when it refers to something in the past (for instance, "play" becomes "played," "walk" becomes "walked") and then she applies this rule to irregular verbs such as "gone," "went," "drank," and "hit." Overregularization demonstrates that your child does not passively reflect the speech she hears every day; instead, she formulates rules about language and then actively tries to apply them to the words she knows. From early on in life, therefore, she tries to develop her own understanding of grammar, but at this age she makes mistakes.

Psychologists have also paid close attention to a child's use of prepositions such as "in" or "on," which describe positional relationships between objects, rather than describing everything in relation to herself. Studies have found that children tend to acquire prepositions in a specific order, reflecting their steadily increasing understanding of the world around them. Typically, the first preposition to appear in your child's vocabulary will be "in," closely followed by the word "on." After that, the order of appearance will probably be "under,"

Above As your child's imagination develops she will love holding pretend telephone conversations, especially if you join in the game.

25 – 30 months

then "beside" and "between." Concepts such as "front" and "back," "before" and "after" don't appear in her speech until much later.

Right Help your child learn the concept of prepositions by encouraging her to describe where she is, in this case under the table.

THE MAIN CHANGES TO LOOK FOR:

● **Questions** Your child discovers that questions serve a number of psychological purposes. For instance, a question enables her to acquire more information about a particular topic without having to investigate it herself; she learns through questions. Questions also give her a sense of empowerment because they put her in a dominant position—she chooses what to ask. There is no specific order in which your child starts to use who, what, how, where, and why questions.

● **Vocabulary** Estimating the vocabulary of a child aged 30 months is extremely difficult. Those researchers who have tried to do so have found that the typical child in this age group has between 100 and 300 separate words. Your child's vocabulary centers around things that matter to her in life, such as her family, her friends, her pet animals at home, food, and familiar objects. The words she uses are more to do with the name of objects and people than their characteristics.

● **Memory** Most children this age are able to recall earlier experiences, such as the shopping trip they went on yesterday, and to describe them to a parent. This represents a huge step forward in your child's understanding and expression. She tells you about things that happened a few moments ago (for instance, that she hurt her hand while playing in the next room) or she casually mentions an incident that happened earlier that day while she was at day care.

● **Imagination** Now that her understanding of symbolism has developed (in that she can use one object to represent another), a whole new range of language opportunities arise. For instance, if she is given a plastic toy telephone, she chats away to the "other person" as if someone is really at the other end of the telephone. Or maybe she chats to her doll or teddy bear as if they are participating in the conversation. It's her imagination that lets her use language in these different ways.

Talking Over You
Your child doesn't like you to disagree with her, and she believes that if she talks over you then her views will carry more weight. So when you tell her that she can't have another cookie, don't be surprised if she immediately repeats her request in a louder voice. This isn't rudeness; she truly thinks that if she says something loud enough, she'll get her own way. Don't try to shout her down, however. Let her have her say, then say your comments once again. Repeat this process as often as necessary. She'll probably grow angry with you and try to talk over you, but don't give in. Wait for a pause in her remarks and then clearly say your point of view again.

Body Language
Subtle Changes

Now that he's in his third year, your child's body language begins to resemble the body language of an adult. Of course, his nonverbal communication remains relatively immature, but you will notice more common ground between his body language and yours. New dimensions of body language emerge at this stage and the existing ones become more complex.

Here are some examples of these changes:

● **Body posture** Position and posture is very effective in nonverbal communication. For instance, if your child places himself before you, hands on hips and head held back, this usually indicates anger or determination; if he leans forward while sitting in a chair, head resting on his cupped hands, this probably tells you he is interested.

● **Hand and arm gestures** These can convey underlying meaning in a very subtle way. For instance, if he brings his hand up to his face to cover his mouth, he is probably surprised or shocked by something; if he suddenly starts to scratch the back of his neck or the top of his head while talking to you, he probably feels embarrassed or anxious.

● **Facial expression** He now has unlimited ways to express emotions through the look on his face. For instance, if his head is tilted slightly to the side and he makes good eye contact with you, then he is listening to what you say and agreeing with you; if his mouth is slightly upturned at one corner, you should assume he is not pleased with whatever is happening.

Below This little girl's increasing level of interest in the dollhouse is demonstrated by her inclined body posture and the expression of concentration on her face.

25 – 30 months

COMFORTERS

Between the ages of 25 and 30 months, your child may have a favorite soft toy that he loves snuggling up to—and it is probably one that he's had since he was a baby. Or maybe he clings to a remnant from an old crib blanket. It's the familiar feel, smell, and even taste of the object that appeals to him. He knows exactly what it will be like to hold and this reassures him. Some children develop the habit of pulling gently at their earlobe when they are tired, ready for sleep. Others suck their thumb while watching television in the evening.

Psychological research reveals that the majority of children of this age have some type of comfort object or comfort habit like this. The term "comforter" is used to describe this sort of phenomenon because it makes your child feel comfortable. This form of nonverbal communication tells you that he is relaxed or that he wants to be relaxed.

Psychologists don't know why children have an emotional need for comforters. It's not a sign of insecurity, because insecure children do not need a comforter more than secure children—almost every child has a comforter sometimes. In fact, the results of psychological studies reveal that a child who has a comforter when he is young is likely to have better relationships with other children once he starts school, and he is less likely to be shy. Using a comforter might actually be good for your child, such as when he is in a strange bedroom on vacation and scared about his new surroundings or anxious about visiting somewhere.

Above Thumb-sucking is one of the most common sources of comfort and typically appears at this age.

Length of Eye Contact

Studies have found that on average the eye contact between parent and child during a conversation is two seconds—after that, one of them breaks the visual link. Then after another few seconds, eye contact is restored. When you and your child speak to each other, you probably make eye contact for only about 35 percent of the time. During the listening phase of the conversation, he looks at you for roughly 75 percent of the total time. A drop in this level of eye contact signals your child's underlying feelings. The most common reason for a reduction in the amount of eye contact he makes during your discussions is that he is worried, nervous, or even feels guilty about something he has done.

Left Rubbing his eyes is one of the clearest indications that your child is tired. This is often a very useful signal for parents.

Top Tips to Help Your Child

Encourage Talking

- **Listen to her tales of adventure** Life is very exciting for your child and she is desperate to tell you everything that happens to her. Harness this zest for life by listening intently to her tales. When she is excited about a particular incident, try to reflect that feeling in your own response. And ask her basic questions about things that have taken place.

- **Encourage speech planning** Your child's initial reaction is probably to tell you about an incident as quickly as possible, without pausing to give you key details. This is typical for a child this age, but you can help her by reminding her to give the names of the children involved or to explain why she was in that situation in the first place.

- **Take her to parent-and-toddler group or nursery school** Social contact with her peers remains one of the most effective ways to boost her speech and language development. Through playing with others her own age, she spontaneously uses spoken language more frequently. Her desire to communicate with them spurs her on to speak as much as she can to her peers.

- **Make music together** Give her a set of toy musical instruments and join in as she tries to create a tune of her own. Your child doesn't need to have any musical ability to take part in this activity. Once she blows the wind instruments and bangs the drum, start to sing along to the sounds made. She'll sing with you.

- **Have structured telephone conversations** Now when you have pretend telephone conversations with your child, add a touch of structure and formality. For instance, open the conversation by saying "hello," then ask to speak to your child by name, and finish by saying "good-bye," just as you would if you were talking to her on a real telephone. This makes her feel very grown-up and she loves it.

- **Ask her to sort** Make a pile of, say, three types of objects, such as wooden blocks, soft toys, and crayons. Mix all these objects together and ask her to give you all the blocks. This is a complex task that involves classification and she may struggle at first. If she selects a wrong item, simply put it back in the pile and ask her again.

- **Demonstrate prepositions** When talking to your child, make a point of using prepositions in your speech and demonstrating their meaning physically. For instance, when she watches you put something on the table, say to her, "I'm putting this on the table," putting special stress on the word "on"; do the same with the words "in" and "under." Demonstrations improve understanding.

25 – 30 months

Use and Interpret Body Language

- **Suggest imaginative play** Your child has great fun dressing up. Watch her during this type of play and you'll notice that her body language is quite different when she pretends, for instance, to be you from when she pretends to be one of her friends. The different roles she plays allows her to practice new ways of communicating nonverbally.

- **Cuddle up during storytime** Make a specific point of putting your arm around your child as you read her a story. Warm body contact adds to her enjoyment of the reading experience, making it much more memorable. This is a good way of using body language to communicate your feelings of love and care toward your child. She'll reciprocate.

- **Balance her use of a comforter** Although a comforter is perfectly acceptable at this age, try to keep your child from becoming too dependent on it, for instance refusing to go outside without her cuddly teddy bear. That's when the comfort object becomes a hindrance, not a help. Be prepared to set limits on when she can access her comforter.

- **Ask her to interpret** True, she's still very young, but she is capable of interpreting facial expressions and other aspects of body language, even if she's not right all the time. Watch a television program with your child. Wait for a scene in which there is someone who doesn't speak, then ask your child if that character is happy or sad.

- **Start to teach manners** Now is a good time to explain about politeness. For instance, tell your child that it's not nice to snatch a toy from another child's hand, nor is it pleasant to push to the front of a line. She might not realize the negative effect of these gestures and depends on you to point this out to her.

- **Sit with her** You might be surprised at how reassured your child is simply by your silent presence. When she is upset or sad or sitting very quietly on her own, go and sit beside her. You don't need to say a word, just be there with her. That gesture on its own may be enough to make her feel better about things.

- **Watch out for new fears** At this age, many children start to develop new temporary fears, even though they are calm and confident in most situations. Fear of darkness is particularly common. The tension expressed in your child's body language when she approaches a darkened room or when you turn her bedroom light off tells you that she is afraid.

Toys Plastic human figures and small plastic buildings ● dolls and a dollhouse ● box of your old clothes for dressing up ● toy zoo with wooden or plastic animals ● lots of storybooks ● music tapes and musical instruments ● toy telephones ● toy cars and garage ● imitation household utensils and appliances ● construction bricks ● arts and crafts materials, including crayons, paper, cardboard, and glue

123

Questions and Answers

Q I've noticed that my child, who is 30 months old, talks with a lisp. What should we do? I'm worried that other people will start to laugh at him.

A Do absolutely nothing at the moment, because the lisp he has is a normal speech characteristic that will disappear without any help. He lisps (that is, he substitutes the sound "f" for "th" and the sound "th" for "s") because he isn't developmentally ready to make the appropriate sound. He probably doesn't realize he has a lisp and may become distressed if you try to explain this to him. Instead, speak to him normally, let him reply with his lisp, and make no comment about his speech errors. Within a few months, the lisp will ease.

Q No matter how often I ask my child questions about the games he has played or the videos he has watched, he gives very sparse replies. How can I encourage him to tell me more?

A As you have already discovered, you cannot force your growing child to speak; you can only try to create an atmosphere at home in which spoken language plays a large part. Any confrontation with him over this issue will probably decrease his communication with you even further. Try a more subtle approach. Keep asking him questions about his activities, and once he has answered, tell him what you did that day. This technique provides him with a model of response that he may imitate eventually.

Q My daughter seems to be talking much sooner than her older brother did. Are girls always faster at learning to speak than boys?

A Results of development surveys have found that, overall, girls tend to acquire language skills at a faster rate than boys. Your everyday experience of your own children and your friends' children probably confirms this in most instances. Nobody is able to offer a full and satisfactory explanation for this gender difference. Remember, however, that every child is different and that some boys talk at a very young age, long before girls the same age have begun to acquire speech. The main point is to do everything you can to encourage your child's progress with speech, whether boy or girl.

25 – 30 months

Q My daughter is 28 months old and her sister is 6 months. I'm sure she loves her, but whenever she plays with her, her body language becomes more assertive and aggressive, and she ends up crying. Could this be a sign that she is jealous?

A That's likely to be an accurate interpretation of her body language, given the current situation at home. After all, like many children, she has conflicting emotions about the new arrival in her family. She probably loves her, but on the other hand she is probably threatened by her presence. She is used to being the center of attention and her sister has now taken that spot away from her. Her aggressive gestures when playing with her are her way of telling you that she feels jealous of her at times.

Q Why does my child sulk when he can't get his own way? He sits in a chair, arms folded, glowering at me, and refuses to talk to me.

A The gestures you describe are his way of telling you that he is annoyed with you. He prefers using nonverbal communication rather than spoken language to say this to you, that's all. Your child hopes that by expressing his disapproval you will change your mind. That would be a mistake, however. Giving in to his demands simply because he uses hostile body language would actually reinforce his actions, making it more likely that he would do the same again in the future. Instead, try to ignore him, or distract him by involving him in another activity.

Q What is the best way to encourage my child to persist? She usually gives up very quickly with a puzzle toy when she can't solve it immediately.

A Her body language tells you that her confidence is low and that she expects to fail. The best way to improve her self-esteem is to help her experience success. The more she succeeds with a puzzle or game, the more her confidence grows. So choose a puzzle toy that you are sure is within her capability. Let her solve it on her own, then give her lots of praise. Next, give her a toy that is only slightly more demanding; help her if necessary. These successes steadily build her enthusiasm, and she'll soon be prepared to try harder.

Development
25–30 Month Skills

MOVEMENT
- Is able to jump a short distance off the ground from a standing position and with practice may be able to jump over a low obstacle.
- Successfully maneuvers herself around obstacles while performing another task. For example, she can push a toy wheelbarrow around the room without crashing into the furniture.
- Is able to take short walks on foot rather than using the stroller.
- Walks up stairs in your house without your support.
- Stands on tiptoes for a couple of seconds.

LANGUAGE
- Adores you reading stories to her just before she goes to sleep.
- Benefits from discussing her activities with you and will get more out of a television program, for example, if you talk about it afterward.
- Asks questions and listens attentively to the answers.
- Has a vocabulary of several hundred individual words.
- Enjoys simple conversations with familiar adults and other children.
- Uses language to extend the complexity of imaginative play, such as dressing up.
- Starts to use pronouns, such as "he" or "you," and prepositions, such as "in" or "on."
- Recalls small amounts of personal information, such as her age and full name, and is able to relate that information.

LEARNING
- Begins to match colors—for example, by finding two bricks of the same color.
- Understands that coins are "money," but still has little concept of value.
- Sorts objects according to specific characteristics. For example, she is able to divide toys according to type—say, animals or cars.
- Begins to develop a broad sense of time and can probably distinguish between "today" and "tomorrow." 
- Identifies herself in a photograph shown to her.
- Is hungry for new experiences beyond the home and enjoys visits to new places such as the zoo or a new park.
- Ascribes human qualities to inanimate objects as an expression of her active imagination and perhaps as a means of understanding the world around her. For example, she may be worried that a favorite toy will be sad if she leaves it at home.

25 – 30 months

HAND–EYE COORDINATION
- Manages to thread large beads on to string or a shoelace.
- When painting and drawing, she grips the crayon or brush with her fingers and is able to make a controlled mark. For example, she may be able to copy a vertical line that you have drawn.
- Copes better with construction toys and games and puzzles that have pieces that fit together.
- Can button and undo large buttons.
- Can start to learn how to use pieces of cutlery other than her spoon.
- Has a firmly established hand preference.

SOCIAL AND EMOTIONAL
- May still be "clingy" when you leave her in someone else's care.
- Starts to learn basic social skills, such as sharing, when playing with siblings and other children.
- Takes an increasingly active part in dressing and undressing. For example, she may pull off her socks and top when getting ready for bed.
- Is more eager to play with other children at times, although arguments are still common.
- Insists on trying more things on her own but may become despondent when she experiences frustration and failure.
- Is prone to temper tantrums when you exert your authority and things don't go her way.

31–36 Months

Your child's spoken language skills rest on a solid foundation of vocabulary, grammar, and meaning, and this provides a good basis for all the subsequent progress he makes with spoken language. Of course, his personality influences the way he uses spoken language (for instance, a shy child says less than an outgoing child), but by the time he is 3 years old he uses language to communicate his feelings and ideas, and to ask questions. Your child's body language has grown more complex; he is aware of himself and his personal space, and he now also uses this to convey his feelings nonverbally.

Language Development
Psychological Factors

Changes in your child's use of spoken language accompany changes in other aspects of her development, too. Young children tend to view the world from their own perspective, often being unable to see beyond their own needs, feelings, and ideas. It's not that they are selfish, just that they haven't yet established a broader outlook on life, and that's one of the main reasons their early speech focuses almost exclusively on themselves. The typical toddler, for example, talks only of herself and her experiences.

The position changes as your child grows toward the end of her third year. Instead of thinking only about herself, she develops awareness that other people in her world have feelings, too, and she becomes concerned about them. Signs of this change in outlook are her distress when she sees you distressed, her attempts to cheer up another child who is crying, and her attempts to please you by giving you one of her drawings. This psychological change is accompanied by a change in her use and content of spoken language. No longer talking solely about herself and her interests, she builds a vocabulary that

Above and left By 36 months children have a good awareness of conversational rules and are able to take turns in a three-way conversation.

130

31 – 36 months

allows her to talk about others and she starts to talk to other people, especially the children she plays with at day care or at home.

Spoken language comes to the forefront as your child's main means of learning. When she was younger, she learned through exploration, through handling toys, looking at them, manipulating them, and even tasting them. Although, that medium of learning will remain important throughout childhood, she now uses spoken language more effectively as a tool of learning. She poses lots of questions, and she likes to have lots of conversations with you, not just to say what she thinks but also to hear your views. Spoken language, therefore, has assumed an enormous importance in her life and will continue to develop rapidly.

THE MAIN CHANGES TO LOOK FOR:

● Conversational rules

Your child is more aware that there are subtle rules about conversations, that it's not a case of blurting out an idea the moment it enters her head. She has long understood the importance of a pause in conversations, but she is more sensitive to other signals that indicate it's her turn to speak, such as when you drop your voice tone slightly at the end of your comments, or when you stop making hand gestures that accompany your speech.

● Hearing and listening

Your child's hearing has matured, enabling her to differentiate a wider range of sounds that she hears every day. Improvement in listening skills is accompanied by greater control over her attention. This means she is able to concentrate better when you talk to her, blotting out other distractions—unless, of course, she makes a deliberate decision to ignore you because she wants to continue watching television!

● Sentence structure

Most times your child is able to express herself using a sentence that follows key grammatical rules and contains at least three or four words. The sentence follows a recognizable sequence and positioning of words, with the noun at the beginning followed by a verb. She uses basic prepositions more frequently and has increased the number of adjectives in her speech. When she is excited, her speech becomes confused.

● Questions

Hardly a day passes without your child seeking an explanation of something she has seen, heard, or thought about. "Who," "how," "where," "when," and "why" regularly start her sentences, depending on what she wants to know. You may even find that she asks the same question that she asked you yesterday. Sometimes she does this for attention. Your child also knows to raise her voice at the end of the question.

Prosodic Factors

Prosodic dimensions of spoken language—for instance, word emphasis, voice intonation, and rate of speech—appear more frequently in your child's language between the age of 31 and 36 months. They allow her to add meaning to the words she uses or to change their meaning altogether. Her recognition of these prosodic influences is a further sign of her growing comprehension. The most common prosodic element used is word emphasis. By the time she reaches the age of 3 years, she knows that stressing one word in a sentence is an effective way of drawing attention to it. Your child might also vary her intonation to make a specific point. Voluntary variation in the rate of speech doesn't appear until she is older.

131

Body Language
Temporary Separations

Perhaps the biggest challenge facing your growing child during this period is learning to cope with temporary separations, whether they occur when you leave him at home with a baby-sitter or with the caregiver in her home, or when you drop him off each morning at day care.

Even though he does not say a word of complaint at these times, his body language might tell you "I'm dreading you leaving me here." By being aware of his separation anxiety, you can give him that extra reassurance and attention to help him cope. Here are some ways he may convey his worry to you nonverbally:

- **Clutches stomach and frowns** The anxiety created by the thought of having to leave you can cause him to experience a genuine headache or sore stomach. He doesn't know this is the cause of his physical discomfort and he does not use this deliberately as a way to foil your plans to go out.

- **Sluggish and lethargic** Separation anxiety can show in the dullness of his responses and general behavior. Most children are excited at attending day care because of all the novel experiences waiting for them there. A change from enthusiasm to lethargy can indicate his fear of leaving you.

- **Slow to get dressed** You may find that somehow his socks are nowhere to be seen when you dress him in the mornings on which he goes to day care, or that the shirt you select for him is never the right one as far as he is concerned. Dressing him, therefore, seems to take ages, even though he dresses quickly on the weekends.

Right General lethargy and a lack of interaction may be a sign that your child is anxious about being separated from you, so give her plenty of reassurance.

Above and right By now children have a fairly sophisticated sense of personal space: the little boy on the left has moved close enough to his friend to show that he is happy to communicate with him.

31 – 36 months

BODY DISTANCE

Your child's growing self-awareness and social skills broaden his understanding of "personal space"—that is, the distance that is comfortably left between himself and the nearest person. The way he changes his body distance gives you insight into his feelings and attitudes at the time.

Psychologists identify four circles of personal space:

- **The intimate circle** This is the area within 18 inches (45 cm) of his body. Only people he knows well are allowed to enter this space—for instance, when he wants you to have a cuddle. In moments of anger, however, he may deliberately bring you into his intimate circle by pushing his furious face into yours.

- **The personal circle** This is the area between 18 inches (45 cm) and 4 feet (1.2 m) from his body, and is the normal distance he maintains between himself and the person he talks to. The personal circle is protective: bringing people into that area is a clear sign that he wants to communicate with them.

- **The social circle** This is the area that lies between 4 feet (1.2 m) and 8 feet (2.4 m) from his body. You'll notice that he leaves this amount of distance when he is uncertain of someone or something. This is his way of communicating the fact that he feels vulnerable.

- **The public circle** This is all the area that is beyond 8 feet (2.4 m) from him, and is generally reserved for such occasions as when he performs in nursery school shows, or for more relaxed moments—for instance, when he proudly recites a newly learned poem to his family or friends.

First Impressions Count

Like it or not, people judge others on their first impressions, even though that may not be accurate. That's why it is important for your child to make a positive impression when he meets new peers for the first time—especially because overturning a bad first impression is difficult.

Research has found that the features of body language often used to make a first impression are facial appearance (for instance, if he smiles or scowls), body posture (if he holds his shoulders back confidently or lets them slump), hand position (if he lets his hands dangle by his side or clenches them nervously), and body distance (if he moves into the personal circle or maintains the social circle).

133

Top Tips to Help Your Child

Encourage Talking

● **Challenge her** Keep your child talking, whether you ask her questions, encourage her to express an opinion, or discuss something that happened to her earlier in the day. It really doesn't matter what you talk about just as long as you keep the dialogue going. The more language experience your child has, the more competent she becomes with speech.

● **Explain the meanings of words** A child this age has the knack of asking her parent to explain words that are in everyday usage yet are very hard to define. Try to explain the meaning of, say, the word "sarcastic" to a 3-year-old. She has heard you use it, but it's a difficult concept to grasp at that age. Be patient with her.

● **Broaden her play experiences** Remember that the more she plays with other children in a variety of social settings, the more language she uses. In addition to day care or nursery school, arrange for other children to visit your house to play with her, and encourage her to accept invitations to any children's parties. There may also be a suitable sports class she could attend.

● **Introduce tongue twisters** The typical 3-year-old loves trying to recite tongue twisters such as "Peter Piper," though she may become frustrated if she finds this too difficult. It's important to encourage her to say the phrase very slowly at first and then gradually speed up. She'll be pleased with any progress that she makes.

● **Step up the quality of her storybooks** Your child is ready for more demanding plots, instead of simple stories that are very repetitive. Don't forget to ask her afterward if she liked the story, and to recall the names of the main people in it. Have her sit beside you so that she can follow the words as you point to them.

● **Discuss her paintings with her** In many instances, you won't have a clue what her drawing represents, even though she has a clear idea. So ask her to tell you about the picture, and about the people, objects, and animals in it. Of course, your child's description probably seems totally remote from the images you see in front of you, but listen attentively.

● **Extend her understanding of comparatives** Show her, for example, a large bowl and a small bowl. Use the appropriate adjective to describe each bowl as you point to it, then ask your child to point to the large bowl or the small one. Do this with other comparatives such as "fat" and "thin" and "long" and "short."

31–36 months

Use and Interpret Body Language

- **Demonstrate personal space** For instance, when she is angry with you and stands very close in an attempt to intimidate you into doing what she wants, gently move her back and tell her that you are uncomfortable being so close to her when she is in a bad mood. This helps her to understand the importance of personal space for others, too.

- **Manage separations calmly** Don't forget that your child reads your body language. This means that if you are tense and worried when leaving her with her baby-sitter or at day care, she'll have no difficulty in interpreting this accurately—and before you know it, she will be anxious, too. She'll copy your calmness if that's what she reads from your body language.

- **Improve positive body language** Other children will relate better to her if she smiles during their conversations, if she nods when she agrees with them, and if she tilts her head slightly to one side when listening to them. These basic social skills make the speaker feel important and valued. Practice this form of body language with her at home so that she becomes more comfortable with doing it naturally.

- **Praise caring gestures** Make a big fuss over your child when you see her act supportively to another child, perhaps when she wipes away that child's tears or when she shares her sweets with the others. These nonverbal acts of pro-social behavior should be encouraged, and the best way to do this is by letting her know that you approve.

- **Watch for rapid changes in body language** Most normal developmental changes are gradual, not sudden—rapid transformations can indicate that there is an underlying emotional concern. An unexpected change from body language that, say, tells you she is very confident to body language that lets you know she is insecure may be her way of telling you she faces a difficult challenge.

Toys Soft toys and dolls for imaginative play ● sing-along cassette tapes and CDs ● selection of children's books ● child-sized kitchen with plastic cups and saucers ● toy people figures with vehicles ● color and shape-matching games ● larger jigsaw puzzles with several pieces ● dress-up outfits with clothes and hats ● child's table and chair ● creative art materials ● plastic railway set with tracks ● bat and ball ● sit-on pedal toy

- **Support her through shyness** Your child's fragile self-confidence is easily shattered. She may have been outgoing and effusive yesterday but today she might cling to you tightly, afraid to let go of you when you try to take her to a party. Try not to become annoyed, even though her shyness interferes with your schedule. Instead, tell her how the others like her.

- **Reduce visual distractions** Her eye contact is less intense when you talk to her while the television or music blares loudly in the same room. Her eyes are naturally drawn to these other sources of stimulation, decreasing her attention to you. You'll find that she makes eye contact for longer if there is less competition from distractions.

Questions and Answers

Q My child wants to learn nursery rhymes but seems to have difficulty memorizing them. How can I help him?

A The best way to memorize any rhyme, poem, or song is in small sections at a time. It could be that your child tries to memorize too much all at once, finds this far too much for his limited memory capacity, and therefore manages to retain only part of it. Teach him a more effective strategy. Encourage him to repeat out loud perhaps only the first half of the line (making sure that each unit he memorizes makes sense on its own). Once he knows this fully after a few days, move on to the next small chunk. In this way, he slowly learns the whole poem.

Q My child is almost 3 years old. A couple of times recently he has woken up during the night crying and upset. Does this mean he is troubled about something?

A Most children have bad dreams occasionally. This is normal. However, when these become more regular, this pattern of behavior can mean there is a deeper underlying anxiety. Think about what is happening in your 3-year-old's life at the moment. Perhaps he isn't getting on well with his friends, or maybe he is concerned that activities at day care are too challenging for him. Talk to him to ascertain if there is something that particularly worries him. Once you have provided him with reassurance, you will probably find that his nights become restful once again.

Q At what age do children start to have a sense of humor?

A Your child's sense of humor begins very early on, in the first few months of life, when she shows her first smile in response to yours. This is proof that she can be amused by something that she sees or hears. As she grows older, her humor changes. By the time she is around 3 years of age, she finds lots of things funny. Mostly, however, she laughs at spontaneous incidents that occur around her, even though you might not find them at all funny. For instance, she giggles when she hears someone say a particular word, or she chuckles loudly when she sees you drop something on the kitchen floor by accident.

31 – 36 months

Q My child is almost 36 months. Is this too young for him to start to learn about numbers?

A Genuine understanding of numbers usually doesn't develop until around the age of 4 or 5 years, but you can lay the foundations for mathematics even at this age. When you walk with your child up and down stairs, slowly count each step. Saying the numbers "one," "two," and so on as you move draws his attention to these words. Do the same when you hand him sweets, or count the fingers on his hand before tickling his palm. You'll probably find that he soon starts to imitate you, by repeating the number names himself.

Q What are "pacifying gestures"?

A These are specific features of your child's body language that convey a feeling of peacefulness and friendliness, in the same way that some gestures of body language convey aggression. Pacifying gestures at this age usually involve hand and arm movements only. They include clapping at another child's actions (a recognized sign of approval), extending a helping hand to another child who has fallen over (proof that there are no underlying feelings of hostility), and sharing (a clear demonstration of his desire to include the other child). A child who uses pacifying gestures like this usually experiences less tension in his social relationships, and consequently tends to bicker less with his pals.

Q Is it possible to use my child's body language to know if he is telling me a lie?

A Interpreting body language is by no means an exact science, so you can't develop a foolproof method of detecting lies using his body language. However, there may be giveaway signs. His inability to make eye contact when telling you something or offering you an explanation is a potential indicator of lying. He may also be very restless as he speaks, fidgeting with his hands and moving his weight from one foot to the other. Some children's cheeks start to redden when they lie to their parent. It comes down to knowing your own child and the way he expresses guilt and discomfort through nonverbal communication.

Development

31–36 Month Skills

MOVEMENT
- Jumps from a small height, such as a single step, without losing her balance.
- Will attempt challenging balancing activities such as walking along a log or hopping, although she may not succeed.
- Balances for several seconds while standing on one foot only.
- Tiptoes across the floor without overbalancing.
- Is able to negotiate ladders and slides on large outdoor play equipment.
- Runs fast with great confidence.
- Can use the pedals of a pedal toy to propel herself along.
- Can accurately copy movements and participate fully in action songs.
- Is steady enough to hold a baby brother or sister on her knee with supervision.

LANGUAGE
- Issues instructions confidently to you.
- Often uses pronouns such as "I" and "me," although not always correctly.
- Has a vocabulary of at least a thousand words.
- Is capable of jumping from one topic to another in conversations.
- Is ready for more complex stories with multiple characters, and likes to listen to adult conversations.
- Enjoys hearing the same story over and over again.
- Asks frequent questions about the meaning of unfamiliar words that she has heard you or others use.
- Shows an understanding of grammatical rules.
- Displays increasing fluency in speech, though words are frequently mispronounced and lisping can be common.

LEARNING
- Compares two objects in terms of size or height, albeit not always accurately.
- Makes up simple stories from her imagination.
- Remembers something you both did yesterday and may be able to recall other exciting events from the more distant past.
- Anticipates the consequences of her actions; she knows that if she knocks her cup over, the drink spills.
- Is able to commit information, such as the name of an object, to memory by repeating it to herself.
- Constantly asks questions about the world around her, such as the following: What? Where? How? Why?

31–36 months

HAND–EYE COORDINATION
- Benefits from the wider range of play equipment and craft activities at a day care or nursery school.
- Is able to build a tower of eight or more blocks.
- Begins to be able to cut paper with a pair of child-safe scissors, although she finds this difficult.
- Completes jigsaw puzzles with three or four large pieces.
- Because of improved control, her drawings are less random and their subject is often recognizable. She can copy simple shapes you draw.
- Carries out simple household tasks like putting utensils on the table or toys in a box.

SOCIAL AND EMOTIONAL
- Has a distinct sense of self and is protective of her possessions and personal space.
- Is clean and dry during the day.
- May form a special friendship with one child in particular.
- More aware of other people's feelings and makes efforts to offer help and comfort to another child who is distressed.
- Becomes more confident in new situations and in forming relationships outside the immediate family.
- Is more amenable to family rules, and tantrums diminish in frequency.
- Enjoys exercising choice over what to eat or wear.

Index of Age Groups

0–3 months 20–31
   body language 24–5, 27
   development chart 30–1
   language development 22–3
   questions and answers 28–9
   talking 26
   tips 26–7
   toys 27
1 month 23, 30–1
1 week 23, 30–1
2 months 23, 30–1
3 months 23, 30–1
4 months 35, 42–3
4–6 months 32–43
   body language 36–7, 39
   development chart 42–3
   language development 34–5
   questions and answers 40–1
   talking 38
   tips 38–9
   toys 39
5 months 35, 42–3
6 months 35, 42–3
7 months 47
7–9 months 44–55
   body language 48–9, 51
   development chart 54–5
   language development 46–7
   questions and answers 52–3
   talking 50
   tips 50–1
   toys 51

8 months 47
9 months 47
10 months 59, 66–7
10–12 months 56–67
   body language 57, 60–1, 63
   development chart 66–7
   language development 58–9
   questions and answers 64–5
   talking 62
   tips 62–3
   toys 63
11 months 59, 66–7
12 months 59, 66–7
13 months 71
13–15 months 68–79
   body language 72–3, 75
   development chart 78–9
   language development 70–1
   questions and answers 76–7
   talking 74
   tips 74–5
   toys 75
14 months 71
15 months 71
16–18 months 80–91
   body language 84–5, 87
   development chart 90–1
   language development 82–3
   questions and answers 88–9
   talking 86
   tips 86–7
   toys 87

19–21 months 92–103
   body language 96–7, 99
   development chart 102–3
   language development 94–5
   questions and answers 100–1
   talking 98
   tips 98–9
   toys 99
22–24 months 104–15
   body language 108–9, 111
   development chart 114–15
   language development 106–7
   questions and answers 112–13
   talking 105, 110
   tips 110–11
   toys 111
25–30 months 116–17
   body language 120–1, 123
   development chart 126–7
   language development 118–19
   questions and answers 124–5
   talking 122
   tips 122–3
   toys 123
31–36 months 128–39
   body language 132–3, 135
   development chart 138–9
   language development 130–1
   questions and answers 136–7
   talking 134
   tips 134–5
   toys 135

General Index

A

action rhymes 39, 71
action words 70
actions and outcomes 39
active emotional body language 85
active nonemotional body language 85
adventures 122
aggression 65, 88
alertness 22
anger 85, 88, 96, 109, 120
anticipation 63
anxiety 36, 51, 97, 132, 136
arguments 75

attention 86, 112
   parent's 62, 110
   skills 34, 38, 59
audience 63

B

babbling 33, 34, 45, 52, 58
baby talk 29
baby-sitters 65, 132
bad dreams 136
ball games 15
bathtime 41
behavior
   better 100

   disruptive 112
   pro-social 135
behavioral prompts 39
better behavior 100
bilingualism 16–17
birth 23
body distance 133
body language 12–13, 21
   0–3 months 24–5, 27
   4–6 months 36–7, 39
   7–9 months 48–9, 51
   10–12 months 57, 60–1, 63
   13–15 months 72–3, 75
   16–18 months 84–5, 87
   19–21 months 96–7, 99
   22–24 months 108–9, 111

25–30 months 120–1, 123
31–36 months 132–3, 135
active 85
changes 135
exaggerated 87
hostile 125
interpretation 12, 27
parents 60, 112
passive 85
positive 135
reflecting 99
responding 72
stimulating 14
body movements 24
body parts, naming 74, 86, 106
body posture 120
books 134
    picture 11, 39, 50
    see also stories
boredom 88, 97
breathing 13

C

calming 51, 110, 111
caregivers 132
caring gestures 135
challenges 75, 134
changes, body language 135
choices 87
chuckling 35, 84
clapping 137
classification 122
clingy child 96
colic 40
color naming 89
comforters 121, 123
communication 38
comparatives 134
complicated tasks 108
comprehension 47
concentration 63, 88, 97, 109
confidence 61, 108–9
confrontation 17, 62, 85
confusion 16
consonant differentiation 22
consonant-vowel sounds 34, 58, 59
contentedness 22
context 10
conversations 26, 34, 93, 95, 96, 97, 117, 131
    pauses 38, 99
    rules 130, 131
cooing sounds 26
core language 17
correction 86
creativity 95

crib blankets 121
criticism 113
crying 13, 25
    4–6 months 36
    colic 40
    interpretation 28
    night 136
    separation 65
    stories 113
    taking seriously 27
crying sensitivity 22
cuddles 39, 63, 96, 109, 111, 123
curiosity 36, 37, 49, 73
current experience 98

D

daily routines 14
delay, bilingualism 16
determination 52, 85
development charts
    0–3 months 30–1
    4–6 months 42–3
    7–9 months 54–5
    10–12 months 66–7
    13–15 months 78–9
    16–18 months 90–1
    19–21 months 102–3
    22–24 months 114–15
    25–30 months 126–7
    31–36 months 138–9
dialogue 34
diapers, changing 24, 25
differences 74
disapproval 112, 125
discomfort 72
disdain 97
disruptive behavior 112
distance 13
doctors 18
dominance, bilingualism 16
dressing 132
dressing up 75, 123

E

embarrassment 120
emotional attachment 25, 48, 64
emotional development see development charts
emotional drives 61
emotional skills 14
emotions see feelings
enjoyment 71, 84
environment 11
environmental awareness 38

errors 100, 110, 118
    speech 124
exaggerated body language 87
examples 62
excitement 101, 110
experience, watching your child 13
experimenting 94
explanations, word meanings 134
exploration 49
expressive language 11
expressive techniques 82
eye contact 13, 26, 87, 101, 121, 135
eye movements 36

F

facial emotions 37
facial expressions 13, 24, 27, 39, 111, 120
    bizarre 76
    interpreting 123
familiar objects 47, 70
familiar people 47
family meals 110
fathers, playing with 77
favorite soft toys 121
fear 75, 97, 113, 123
    of darkness 123
feelings 12, 24, 37, 60, 76, 129, 130
    expressing 72–3
    negative 49, 72, 84
    positive 49, 72, 84, 111
    reflecting 27
first impressions 133
first language 17
first words 53, 57, 58, 59, 64, 69, 77, 82
food, flicking 112
friendships 108
frowning 40, 73
frustration 53, 61, 107
fun 14, 71, 111
function words 70
funny faces 63

G

games
    ball 15
    listening 38, 98
    peek-a-boo 51
    tickling 27
    word 47
gazing 61, 63
gender differences 53, 124
general nominals 70

gestures 48–9, 74, 84–5, 99, 120
   pacifying 137
   socially inappropriate 100
grammar 10
grammatical rules 105, 118
grammatical structure 106
group situations 15
grumpiness 49
guidelines 18

H

hand and arm gestures 120
hand–eye coordination 14
   see also development charts
happy disposition 12
headaches 132
hearing 18, 19, 41, 47, 131
   aids 19
   loss 47
helping hand 137
holistic approach 14
holophrases 58
hostile body language 125
hostile touch 109
hugs see cuddles
human sounds 22
humor 63, 136
hunger 25

I

ideas 49, 60, 129
ill-health 37
imagination 119
imaginative play 123
imitation 25, 50, 52
independence 15, 61, 75, 88
inflections 106
instructions 59, 83, 85, 98
interest 120
   expression 24, 34
interpretation, body language 12, 27
intimate circle 133
intonation 58, 131
   awareness 22
investigation 49

J

jealousy 125
joining in 71
jokes 83

L

language
   expressive 11
   grammar 10
   meaning 10
   receptive 11
   sounds 10
   see also body language;
      development charts; spoken
      language
language development 11
   0–3 months 22–3
   4–6 months 34–5
   10–12 months 58–9
   13–15 months 70–1
   16–18 months 82–3
   19–21 months 94–5
   22–24 months 106–7
   25–30 months 118–19
   31–36 months 130–1
   difficulties 18–19
   see also development charts
language use 12
laughing 35, 39, 60, 83, 136
learning 100, 131
   parent's 28
   skills 14, 18, 19
   see also development charts
legs 13
lethargy 132
lifting head and shoulders 36
lighting 19
linguistic curiosity 107
lip and tongue movements 110
lisping 124
listening 19, 35, 62, 71
   games 38, 98
   gestures 99
   skills 23, 34, 74, 83, 131
love 51
loving gestures 51
loving touch 109, 111
lying 137

M

majority language 16
manners 123
massage 51
mealtime discussions 110
meaning 10
   understanding 35
meaningful phrases 95
memorizing rhymes 136
memory 117, 119

skills 46
minority language 16
mirrors 35
misery 96
mistakes see errors
mixing socially 19
mobility 108
modifiers 70
movement see development charts
movement skills 14
movements 21, 36
music 35, 38, 98, 122
musical instruments 62
mutual exclusivity bias 71

N

name awareness 41
name recognition 65
naming body parts 74, 86, 106
naming objects 50, 82, 98, 107
naming people 98
nature 11
negative command
   child's 101
   parent's 87
negative feelings 49, 72, 84
negative nonverbal messages 39
negative touch 111
neutral expression 64
noises 83
   talking about 26
nonverbal communication see body
   language
numbers 137
nursery rhymes 136
nursery school 17, 122
nurture 11

O

object permanence 46, 51
objects
   familiar 47, 70
   naming 50, 82, 98, 107
   sorting 122
   whole object bias 71
overextensions 94
overregularization 118

P

pacifiers 64
pacifying gestures 137
paintings 134

palmar grasp 24
parent-and-toddler groups 65, 75, 88, 100, 122
parentese 26
parents
   away during day 77
   linguistic style 82
passive child 64
passive emotional body language 85
passive nonemotional body language 85
patience 63, 74, 82
pauses, conversations 38
peek-a-boo games 51
people, naming 98
persistence 52, 125
personal circle 133
personal social words 70
personal space 132, 135
personality 29, 64
phonology 10
phrases 81, 83, 93, 94, 95
picture books 11, 39, 50
picture identification 95
playing 25, 49, 134
   fathers 77
   imaginative 123
   pretend 74, 86
   water 39
pleasure, showing 38
pointing 89
   pictures 39
poking 73
positive body language 135
positive feelings 49, 72, 84, 111
positive mutual gazing 61
positive response 74
positive strategies 18
postures 13
potty training 108
pragmatics 10
praise 98, 135
prepositions 118, 122
pretend play 74, 86
pro-social behavior 135
professionals 18, 19
progress 16
pronouns 118
pronunciation 95, 100
prosodic factors 131
psychological factors 130–1
psychological studies, bilingualism 17
public circle 133
pulling earlobes 121
pulling hands 73
puzzles 49

Q

questions 117, 119, 129, 131
   asking 50
   posing 38
questions and answers
   0–3 months 28–9
   4–6 months 40–1
   7–9 months 52–3
   10–12 months 64–5
   13–15 months 76–7
   16–18 months 88–9
   19–21 months 100–1
   22–24 months 112–13
   25–30 months 124–5
   31–36 months 136–7
quiet babies 29
quiet times 98

R

rate of speech 101, 131
reading stories 38, 62, 86, 113, 123
receptive language 11
referential techniques 82
reflecting body language 99
reflecting feelings 27
reflex actions 24
rejection 37
relaxation 15, 24, 101, 121
repetition 19, 82
representation 46
responding 26, 27
   body language 72
   cuddles 63
rules 87

S

saliva bubbles 50, 110
saying no *see* negative command
searching 51
second language 17
self-absorption 130
self-confidence 125, 135
   parent's 28
self-consciousness 96
self-directing speech 89
self-esteem 125
self-referring speech 107
sentences 93, 94
   structure 131
separation anxiety 132
separations 65, 132, 135

sex differences *see* gender differences
sharing 137
shouting 76
shyness 96, 99, 135
siblings 76
   comparisons 53
sight 19
silence 96–7, 99
singing 14, 26, 27, 47, 50, 62, 83, 98, 113
single words 81
sitting up 37
sitting with child 123
sloping body posture 73, 120
sluggishness 132
small groups 15
smiling 28
social circle 133
social contact 93
social conversation 34
social development *see* development charts
social gestures 63, 111
social interactions 49
social opportunities 75, 87, 134
social rules 10, 38
social skills 14
socially inappropriate gestures 100
soothing 25, 26, 87
   words 11
sorting objects 122
sound combinations 45
sound differentiation 34, 47
sounds 10, 21, 33, 35
sparse replies 124
special needs 18–19
specific nominals 70
speech 108
   errors 124
   planning 122
   sounds 19
speech and language therapists 19
spoken language 69, 129
   stimulating 14–15
   see also development charts; language
stance 13
staring 23, 73
startle reflex 24
stimulation 14–15
stomachaches 132
stories 107, 110
   crying 113
   reading 38, 62, 86, 113, 123
   talking about 74
   see also books
studying expressions 51

143

stuttering 112
sulking 84, 125
surprise 120
syllable combinations 58
syntax 10

T

talking 28
   0–3 months 26
   4–6 months 38
   7–9 months 50
   10–12 months 62
   13–15 months 74
   16–18 months 86
   19–21 months 98
   22–24 months 105, 110
   25–30 months 122
   31–36 months 134
   about stories 74
   interpret gestures 74
   to child 62
   to himself 89
talking over you 119
tantrums 84, 85, 87, 109
taxonomic bias 71
teaching concepts 19
telegraphic speech 106–7
telephone conversations 86, 118, 122
television 29, 50
temporary separations 132
third-party instructions 98
threats 100
thumb-sucking 121
tickling 35

games 27
time 17
   giving child 86
timing 18
tips
   0–3 months 26–7
   4–6 months 38–9
   7–9 months 50–1
   10–12 months 62–3
   13–15 months 74–5
   16–18 months 86–7
   19–21 months 98–9
   22–24 months 110–11
   25–30 months 122–3
   31–36 months 134–5
tone variation 26
tongue projection 109
tongue thrusting 100
tongue twisters 134
touching 73, 85, 111
toys 19
   0–3 months 27
   4–6 months 39
   7–9 months 51
   10–12 months 63
   13–15 months 75
   16–18 months 87
   19–21 months 99
   22–24 months 111
   25–30 months 123
   31–36 months 135
   brightly colored 19
   favorite 121
   snatching 65
turn taking 26, 97

U

understanding 69
unhappiness 96
unresponsiveness 37

V

verbalize intentions 51
vision 18, 22
visual cues 19
visual distractions 135
vocabulary 57, 70, 83, 95, 107, 117, 119
   explosion 93
   strategy 82
voice recognition 40
vowel differentiation 22

W

walking 60
watching over 111
water play 39
whole object bias 71
womb 23
word bias 71
word combinations 83
word emphasis 131
word games 47
word meanings, explanations 134
word order 106
word patterns 59
words 58, 94
wrong words 83, 86

Acknowledgments

The publisher would like to thank all the children and parents who took part in the photoshoot for this book for their time, energy, patience, and cooperation. We would also like to thank the following companies for allowing us to use their products:

Early Learning Centre, South Marston Park, Swindon SN3 4TJ England
Tel: 01793 831300

Active Birth Centre, 25 Bickerton Road, London N19 5JT England
Tel: 020 74820 5554

Executive Editor Jane McIntosh
Editor Abi Rowsell
Executive Art Editor Leigh Jones
Designer Tony Truscott

Photographer Peter Pugh-Cook
Stylist Aruna Mathur
Production Controller Lucy Woodhead
Picture Researcher Jennifer Veall